D0355082

I dreamed many dreams that never came true,
　　I've seen them vanish at dawn.
But I've realized enough of my dreams, thank God,
　　To make me want to dream on.
I've prayed many prayers, when no answer came
　　Tho I've waited patient, long,
But answers have come to enough of my prayers,
　　To make me keep praying on.
I've trusted many a friend, that failed
　　And left me to weep alone,
But I've found enough of my friends true blue,
　　To keep me trusting on.
I've sown many seed that fell by the way
　　For the birds to feed upon,
But I've held enough golden sheaves in my hand
　　To make me keep sowing on.
I've drained the cup of disappointment in pain
　　And gone many days without song
But I've sipped enough nectar from the roses of life,
　　To make me want to live on.

Fawcett Crest Books
by Dr. Ken Olson:

THE ART OF HANGING LOOSE IN AN UPTIGHT
  WORLD

CAN YOU WAIT TILL FRIDAY?

ARE THERE FAWCETT PAPERBACKS
YOU WANT BUT CANNOT FIND IN YOUR LOCAL STORES?

You can get any title in print in Fawcett Crest, Fawcett
Premier, or Fawcett Gold Medal editions. Simply send title and
retail price, plus 50¢ for book postage and handling for the first
book and 25¢ for each additional book, to:

MAIL ORDER DEPARTMENT,
FAWCETT PUBLICATIONS,
P.O. Box 1014
GREENWICH, CONN. 06830

There is no charge for postage and handling on orders for
five books or more.

Books are available at discounts in quantity lots for industrial
or sales-promotional use. For details write FAWCETT WORLD
LIBRARY, CIRCULATION MANAGER, FAWCETT BLDG.,
GREENWICH, CONN. 06830

CAN YOU WAIT TILL FRIDAY?

The Psychology of Hope

Dr. Ken Olson

A FAWCETT CREST BOOK

Fawcett Publications, Inc., Greenwich, Connecticut

CAN YOU WAIT TILL FRIDAY? The Psychology of Hope

THIS BOOK CONTAINS THE COMPLETE TEXT OF THE ORIGINAL TRADE SIZE EDITION.

A Fawcett Crest Book reprinted by arrangement with O'Sullivan Woodside & Company.

Copyright © 1975 by Kenneth J. Olson

All rights reserved, including the right to reproduce this book or any portions thereof in any form.

ISBN 0-449-23022-8

Printed in the United States of America

10   9   8   7   6   5   4   3   2   1

My cup runneth over because
of a loving wife, Jeannie;
two fine sons, Mike and Dan;
and a wonderful daughter, Jan.

ACKNOWLEDGEMENTS

I am very grateful for all the people who have touched me and helped me grow as a person. I am appreciative of the hard work done by John L. Boonshaft, both as an agent and a friend. In writing this book, I thank Don Demars for his personal contribution; Barbara Wilford, as secretary; and Betty Swanson, who adds the polish to what I write.

Finally, I want to thank you for buying this book, because without you there are no successful authors or books.

CONTENTS

1

CAN YOU WAIT?

Hope is a waking dream.
Aristotle

At 12:30 A.M. on a very early Monday morning I was awakened by the insistent ringing of the telephone. Calls at this time meant only one thing—trouble. From deep sleep I was quickly roused, and I picked up the phone.

My answering service said, "Dr. Olson? This is an emergency, I'll connect you directly with the party."

"Hello. Who is this?"

"Doc? This is Sarah. I've got a rope hung in my bedroom, and I'm going to hang myself tonight."

"Well, why did you wake me up to tell me that? You and I both know you can kill yourself any time you choose, and neither God nor I can stop you if you decide to die. Although you must admit, Sarah, you really don't have any talent for hanging yourself. Remember the last time you hung the rope? You fell off the chair and broke your ribs. You're still taped up! Besides, you're not even in your apartment now. You are in a phone booth outside, on the street."

"How did you know that?"

"Well, I may be sleepy, but I'm not stupid. I know you can't afford a phone, and I can hear by the traffic going by that you're in a phone booth. By the way, I'm scheduled to see you at noon on Friday. Can you wait till Friday to commit suicide? You haven't been eating too well lately, so what kind of a sandwich would you like at Friday noon?"

"What did you say, Doc?"

"Sarah, can you wait till Friday to die? Please tell me what kind of sandwich you would like . . . bologna, ham salad, egg salad, tuna fish, salami?"

"What are you trying to do, Doc?"

"I'm trying to find out if you can wait till Friday to die. We can have one last meal together, and give each other a big hug good-by. Then you can go kill yourself. Now I'd like you to make a decision. What kind of sandwich would you like?"

"Oh, I'll have tuna fish."

"I'll see you Friday at noon." And with that I went back to sleep.

The story of Sarah is so incredible that if I could tell you the whole story of her life, you would have a hard time believing it, much less understanding it. I'll never forget the first day I had an appointment to meet Sarah. Her pastor had called and said his church had decided to pay for her therapy as a part of their social ministry.

Into my office that late afternoon came this very slender, twenty-two-year-old young woman, with a colored handkerchief over her head, sun glasses and bare feet. She was thin, very frightened, and yet knowledgeable about talking with shrinks. She began to tell me part of the story of her life. I never really uncovered the entire story until years later. She stated that she had been hospitalized for psychiatric reasons sixteen times. She was first hospitalized at age thirteen.

I said, "At thirteen? For what?"

"They thought I was a heroin addict. They didn't realize that I didn't even know what heroin was at thirteen. What I was doing was getting hypodermic needles, drawing blood out of my arm and shooting the blood on the wall.

"The day my father found the needles, I said I would run away and the family would never see me again. At first he was furious and told me to go and never come back, but when I was ready to leave he suddenly changed his mind and begged me to stay at home. I did but the next day he had me taken to the state hospital, and they put me in a maximum security ward where I was under constant surveillance.

"My roommate was a woman who was there because she had baked one of her babies to death in the oven, and was stopped before she baked the other one.

"They were sure I was on drugs and thought I was getting heroin into the hospital. I didn't even know what it was! The doctors kept me so sedated that it's no wonder they thought I was on dope. I was, but it was legal dope called medicine.

"When I went to the hospital, I knew this meant I was really bad—so bad I didn't belong to my family any more. I had no right to be a person. I guess that's why I have enjoyed being pregnant the times I have. For the first time I felt like there was something alive in me, even though the rest of me felt dead."

She said she didn't trust doctors. She had been raped by a psychiatrist in the hospital while she was tied down to an examining table, and she had an illegitimate baby by him. I soon learned that she was a very self-destructive person. Her destructive behavior was manifest in the abuse of herself through drugs, alcohol and suicide attempts.

She also had a split personality. Her other person was called Serena. She had been diagnosed a chronic schizophrenic—whatever that means. All the while Sarah was revealing the accounts of her troubled life, I got the distinct impression that I was the one being interviewed and tested, to see how I would react to *her*.

I felt that she presented a real challenge to me and the philosophy that I have—that I never see patients, only people. I asked her if she wanted to change.

"That's why I'm here," she said.

"Just being here is a step in the right direction, but I want you to think about answering this question: Do you want to change your life? *I* can't heal you. You must assume primary responsibility for your life, and the changes that need to be made in it. I'm also wondering if you are ready for someone like me who is very direct and very open. I will not play any therapy games with you. I won't relate to you as doctor to patient, but only as person to person."

I went on to explain my personal philosophy of therapy —that a person gets better faster when he understands that he has the prime responsibility for his life. I would be there as someone who cares, who listens, who offers suggestions and even gives homework assignments. "Sarah, I want you to think very carefully about this for one week. Do you want to change? Can you deal with a person like me?" She agreed to see me in one week.

Sarah would come for her weekly appointments as usual with bare feet and dark glasses. At times she would be so spaced out she would rest her head against the wall and then, with her hands, rub the wood paneling as if to hold onto something real. She was so alone and so terribly frightened, hanging onto life by her fingernails.

The first months were spent trying to establish a relationship where Sarah could begin to trust me and to believe that I cared. There was also the added confusion of speed, hallucinatory drugs, mental disturbance, and the sheer struggle for day-by-day survival.

She was now facing a custody hearing for her eight-month-old daughter who had been placed in a foster home. This happened when it was discovered that she would have to undergo exploratory surgery of the neck for cancer.

The night before surgery I received an urgent call from the pastor who was with Sarah at the hospital. He was frantic. Sarah's other personality, Serena, was there! "What shall I do?" he asked. "Do you have any suggestions, Ken?"

"Sure I do. Put Serena on the phone." I said, "Serena? I'm very angry with you. Why are you frightening Sarah and the pastor by showing up tonight right before surgery? It's very thoughtless of you. Now please get out of there and leave Sarah alone! She is scared enough about the operation, and what will happen to her little girl. She doesn't need you to frighten her any more. Will you leave her alone and go away?"

"Yes," replied a weak little voice.

"Good! Now let me speak to the pastor. I think everything will be all right for now." There are times when I work with people that I feel like an exorcist! Serena was never heard from again.

The surgery, thankfully, revealed no cancer. But when her young daughter was placed in a foster home, welfare department and social workers began to investigate Sarah's being a fit mother and her ability to provide a home. This was a very traumatic time for Sarah. She felt trapped and betrayed. All she had in this world, all that she loved, was her little girl. If you had as little as she had, the thought of losing a child through a court battle was almost too much.

She pleaded with me to write a letter to the welfare department stating that she was a fit mother. I told her I would not write such a letter, because I would not lie. Besides, I would never write *any* letter for her.

"Why not, Doc?"

"Because I believe I have to be the one person that you can finally trust and be open with, and never worry that I'm going to write about you to someone else."

Sarah told me so many different stories about her chaotic life that she became very paranoid every time someone asked her for details of times and places. She was afraid of what they were writing down and what others would believe from hospital records. It soon built a case of absolute hopelessness for her. It was the fear of losing the custody hearing that pushed Sarah to attempt to hang herself, when she fell off the chair and broke her ribs.

One day when she came in for her appointment, she was so confused and stoned she could barely remember where she was. The night before was just a series of blurs. While I looked down at my desk, she said, "I can't even remember where I got this." I looked up to see her pointing a ten-inch hunting knife at me. In all my training, or in the books I have read, I have never been told how to handle such a situation.

I said quickly, "Sarah, I am really angry with you. Don't you realize that when you were so stoned last night, if you had been stopped by the police and they had discovered that big knife hidden on your person, you could have been jailed for carrying a concealed weapon?" And with that, I took the knife out of her hand and slammed it in the desk drawer, needless to say, with a big sigh of relief.

Sarah, a few weeks later said, "I can't stand Phoenix any more. I'm going to split to California. This is just too much. I know I'm going to lose the custody hearing. Do you know any good nut houses in California?"

I replied, "I understand why you want to run—that has been the story of your life. But if you do split, please keep thinking about the question I asked you: Do you want to change? You asked me about hospitals. Well, I was at Napa State Hospital doing some group therapy training. You might check that out if you need a place to stay."

It was before she left for California I received that phone call saying she was going to hang herself, and I asked her if she could wait till Friday.

Sarah did leave, and went to several hospitals. She could talk herself into some of the most expensive private hospitals without a dime to her name. I would periodically receive letters, some of them under fictitious names, like the following:

> *Things are just as mixed up as before .... The first place turned me loose, saying I was merely neurotic .... The second place referred me to a medical hospital, and diagnosed me as having organic brain syndrome. And this third ... is a neuro-psychiatric unit of a hospital .... I'm damned tired of people playing with my mind, and then saying they can't help .... My body is sound and my mind is pretty loose. That's the scope of it. I want to be able to see you as before when I return to Arizona ... I've learned a lot of things on this trip—how to sway with the wind, flow with the current and exercise some patience, listen to my own mind .... Please write, Doc, fly free and be yourself when you answer ....*
>
> > *Peace and Love*
> > *Sarah*

While she was in Utah, she tried suicide once more unsuccessfully, and was placed again in the maximum security ward at a state hospital. Sarah had an amazing ability to be at one moment extremely loose in her associations and thinking processes, and then pull her mind together and focus energies for a moment of time.

She pleaded with them to let her go because she wanted to go back to Phoenix and see her own doctor. They laughed at her for saying she had her own doctor. In her purse she carried a handwritten will, a picture of her daughter and my business card. She said, "This is my doctor, and this is who I want to see."

She finally came back to Phoenix and found a place to rest in a halfway house for rehabilitation of alcoholics. Then she asked for an appointment with me.

When I saw her she looked a great deal better. She had gained back some weight and her mind seemed more together. She said, "I'm ready to answer the question now that you asked me six months ago. I do want to change. I want to be well."

Sarah began the long road back with many detours. One of the most difficult problems she had to contend with was that of the future of her child. She spent one Sunday afternoon with her daughter who stood in a corner and cried, and wanted nothing but to go home to "mommy and daddy." She didn't even remember Sarah. We talked at great length about this experience of rejection by her daughter. It was logical she wouldn't know her because she was only a small baby when Sarah left. Sarah began to realize how happy she was with her foster parents who wanted to adopt her legally.

One of the most significant turning points in her life was to make the decision, on her own, to give her daughter freely to this family who loved her so. It was very hard for her, you must realize, because all she had was her daughter. For Sarah, this marked the beginning of a new stride in her recovery.

I asked Sarah what she thought about during the time that she was on the run and in and out of all the hospitals.

She replied, "The one thought that kept running through my mind was the realization that you cared about me, not as a patient, but as a real person. And when you asked, 'Can you wait till Friday?' it stopped me many times from acting destructively, even though I was doing enough damaging things with all the psychedelic drugs, amphetamines, bartiturates I was using. But still I realize now that my patience will have to be dealt with, and I must learn how to wait. I will tell myself that I can wait one more minute, one more hour, one more day, before I do something stupid again. My nights are still tormented with memories and nightmares, but I know I can make it till morning."

The more I was able to relate openly and honestly with Sarah, the more I was impressed with the beauty of her inner spirit. For in her was a love and gentleness and compassion seldom seen in people. I remember the day she came in with great pride that she had found a job for herself, all by herself. It was as a nurse's aid in the surgery ward of a hospital, and not the best-paid in the the world. Often she would spend what few minutes she could spare sitting with people either before or after surgery. In her own quiet way she would let them know that she cared; that she, too, had been in some frightening situations in her life.

I wish I could say that things always went so well for Sarah, that she continued to grow and become more whole, and that she lived happily ever after. There always seemed to be one more roadblock and one more detour.

One of the problems she was always faced with was the mysterious one of losing her balance. Sometimes she stumbled around like a drunk, although she was not drinking and was not on any drugs. This bothered her and she wondered if it was in her mind.

I tried to have her seek a physician, to have a thorough workup to find out if there was an organic, physical basis for her behavior. I don't think she was afraid of the physical exam, but she hated to fill out those forms on personal history. "Have you ever been treated for a mental disorder? When? Where?" She was very stubborn with me at this point, and it was a long time before I finally got her to see a physician.

The doctor, knowing of her drug behavior in the past, gave her some valium to help her sleep. But Sarah had a history of abusing her body on chemical substances. One time she was brought into a crisis clinic after taking too many valiums, and she had absolutely no control over her muscles. This led to her being hospitalized.

The diagnosis was that she was suffering from myasthenia gravis which affects balance and muscle control. Victims of the disease look like they are drunk, and they stumble and fall. The worst drug of all that she could have been given was a muscle relaxant, which is basically the effect valium has on the body.

Later she was told by another doctor that she didn't have myasthenia gravis.

Sarah didn't like to talk about her symptoms. She finally told me about the general weakness in her muscles. She would go out of her way to find a route where she wouldn't have to exert the energy to lift her foot up over a curb. While taking a shower, it was even hard to wash her hair because it was extremely difficult for her to raise her arms. She had difficulty in swallowing which interfered with her speech. She had to sit up at night to breathe. Even holding her head up took great effort, and she very self-consciously watched that her mouth didn't droop open.

For a period of time Sarah withdrew from me, and I didn't see very much of her. However, I would get an occasional phone call. One time, late at night, I received another call from the answering service. Sarah, in a very weak voice, said, "Doc, I have 140 morphine pills counted out in front of me. What shall I do with them?"

The thought of 140 morphine pills absolutely freaked me out, because I couldn't imagine how an MD, knowing her drug history, would allow her a prescription for morphine.

I said to her very quietly, "Take all the morphine pills and flush them down the toilet. I'll wait." Soon I heard the toilet flush, and she came back to the phone. I said, "Did you get rid of them?"

"Yes," she said, "and I want to see you as soon as possible."

I don't know if you have ever gone through a severe emotional problem, and been hospitalized for psychiatric purposes. It's difficult to find a physician to listen to your physical symptoms without immediately assuming that, because you have a psychiatric history, it's all in your head. It's frustrating for so many who seek help to find someone who will listen and not insist on playing the "God" role. This was happening to Sarah as she went from one doctor to another. I wanted the physician to do just the body work and to leave the head to me.

Finally, in time she came back, and was able to say that she had found a physician who had rediagnosed her myasthenia gravis; that she was on medication and was not abusing it, and that she was doing very well.

Someone once asked Sarah why it was so different now, after all the years she had been in mental institutions and all the many psychiatrists she had seen. Why was her relationship with me so unlike the others? A friend spoke up and said, "Doc never treated Sarah as a patient, but as a person, and he loved her."

I learned a great deal from Sarah. I relearned again the lesson that when I thought there was little or no hope for her life, somebody else still thought she had a chance. This lesson of humility, I must admit, I must periodically relearn, and be brought again down to my knees.

She taught me some valuable theology. One time when we were talking about prayer I confessed that sometimes I felt when I prayed I received no answers. She said, "Don't you know, Doc, God answers prayers through other people."

I also relearned the truth that where there is hope, there is life. She was forever bringing me poems, spiritually philosophical ideas, and books to read to help me grow. I will always be indebted to her for this one:

A Living Faith

I dreamed many dreams that never came true,
I've seen them vanish at dawn.
But I've realized enough of my dreams, thank God,
To make me want to dream on.
I've prayed many prayers, when no answer came
Tho I've waited patient, long,
But answers have come to enough of my prayers,
To make me keep praying on.
I've trusted many a friend that failed
And left me to weep alone,
But I've found enough of my friends true blue,
To keep me trusting on.

I've sown many seed that fell by the way
    For the birds to feed upon,
But I've held enough golden sheaves in my hand
    To make me keep sowing on.
I've drained the cup of disappointment in pain
    And gone many days without song
But I've sipped enough nectar from the roses of life,
    To make me want to live on.

I didn't tell the story of Sarah to demonstrate a technique to be used when talking to a person contemplating suicide. Each person is unique and must so be evaluated. But there was one important message I communicated to Sarah. At her most self-destructive moment, I asked her the question "Can you wait till Friday?"

For some very impulsive and self-damaging people, saying, "Yes, I can wait," one more minute, one more hour, or one more day or week, sometimes buys for them that precious moment that may mean the difference between life and death, between losing and winning, and struggling to become a more alive and responsible person. It can break into that trapped feeling when they are just reacting to life or disappointment, and allows them time to think.

"Can you wait?" became a creed for Sarah to wait one more moment or one more day. It gave her the hope to believe that she could, inch-by-inch and hour-by-hour, make it back to life again, for she had reached the bottom. If she had worried how long the journey would be before she could have a fully functioning life, the distance and energy necessary for such a trip would have been too much for her to conceive. She would have stayed at the bottom; but she learned how to wait, and it gave her a toehold on life.

Emotionally she is doing very fine at present. She's had a setback with myasthenia gravis, but knowing Sarah, she'll still bring joy and hope wherever she is. She is living in another town and is confined to a bed, but she's determined to walk again and give of herself to those less fortunate. We are still in contact with each other.

I wonder how many of you are defeated by the mere contemplation of a very hard and difficult task. Do you worry about how long it will take, how much energy will be expended and what the risks will be—whether or not you have the strength to complete the job? Do you say, "No, I don't," and then give up?

I took a course in medical hypnosis from Milton Erickson, who has done more research on the subject than any other living person. He told a story about a pleasure yacht that exploded in the ocean. No one could get on a life jacket or into a lifeboat. Everyone was in the water in an instant, and the people cried out to the captain, "How far is it to shore?"

He said, "I think it's about fifteen or sixteen miles."

One after another the passengers said, "I can't swim sixteen miles!" so they drowned.

However, the next morning on the beach someone found a half-drowned, but still alive and struggling, fifteen-year-old girl who had this one statement going through her mind, still on her lips, "I know I can swim one more stroke." She never said to herself that she could swim sixteen miles, but she knew she could swim one more stroke. Because she could swim one more stroke—all that she asked of herself—she was finally able to reach her goal—saving her life.

I'm reminded of an old Chinese proverb: "The longest journey begins with but a single step."

There is real power in that sentence. Just think how important it would be if we could learn to wait before we did something habitual, repetitive and destructive to our lives.

I think we live in a very impatient time. We have become very impatient people. We love instant potatoes and instant entertainment. We want to have things done immediately. We can't stand to wait. We get very frustrated, irritable, impatient and explosive. In fact, ask anyone who has worked in the television industry, either as a performer or writer, how it appears that the American public just devours the material and talent they put out and then is still never satisfied. Maybe that is part of our problem—that we are never satisfied. Do we ever have enough? Do we always want more, and more, and more? Once we start eating popcorn, we can't stop.

Sometimes in raising children parents give them the message, "Hurry and grow up." If the child is five, it's too bad he's not seven; or if he's nine, it's a shame he's not eighteen. It's as if we never have the right to be right where we are, and to enjoy the time and the world that we have.

Very often I have seen, as a marriage counselor, young couples who can't wait to catch up to their parents' standard of living. So they go into hock to build a home, buy expensive things, and they spend most of their waking hours working to make payments.

Frankly, I guess too many of us suffer from a serious

psychological problem callen "spoileditis." If we don't get our needs satisfied immediately, we have a tantrum because, after all, "the world owes us a living." We don't know how to deal easily with frustration. We don't know how to wait. When people want to talk about changing some of their bad habits or solving their problems, they say, "I can't wait that long. I can't change. I can't take the time. I can't wait to smoke the next cigarette." It's such a traumatic experience for us that it's almost as if we have to smoke that next cigarette so we can have peace.

There is no one more pious than a reformed smoker or a reformed drunk. I admit that I'm a reformed smoker. It came about because my little daughter Jan cried a lot when I smoked and dumped my cigarettes in the toilet when I brought them home. While I was working in drug abuse control for three years in Phoenix, I would try to talk to young people about the stupidity of destructive addictive behavior. Then I would cough a lot and sputter. Then they'd say, "Yes, Doc, tell us all about it. You know what it's like to be an addict."

We had commitment night. If you wanted to make a non-chemical commitment or a non-smoking commitment, or whatever else, you came before the group. I had a staff of long-haired ex-addicts. They also took a non-smoking commitment for a period of time. This wasn't like a New Year's resolution. When you made a commitment, the group asked you what it would cost you if you broke your commitment. These young longhairs said they would shave their heads bald if they broke theirs. They looked at me and said, "Doc, what about you? You can't shave your head, because you're pretty bald already. You can't grow long hair, so if you break the commitment, what will it cost you?" Then somebody said, "I know what would get him—$200 to the American Cancer Society for one cigarette!" I made that commitment in October 1970 and haven't smoked since then. I realize that I have been given the gift of two clean lungs again.

I used to pride myself on being an athlete. I go every summer to Maui, Hawaii, to teach in dentistry. When I was still smoking, I could hardly swim out to a close reef without feeling like I was going to die for lack of breath. A year later, after I had quit smoking, I could swim for hours. Now I know I am one cigarette away from smoking. If I smoked one cigarette it would push the "on" button in the memory bank of my mind which would activate twenty years of smoking behavior.

I also think we condition ourselves that if we quit smoking, we will gain a lot of weight. That's a mental setup. When you quit smoking, you overeat. You say, "See, I gained a lot of weight, just like I said I would. Now I can go back to smoking so I can lose weight. After all, being overweight is hazardous to my health."

Speaking of being overweight, how many of us have tried to diet and maybe lost thousands of pounds in our lifetime. We put ourselves on a diet that is so bad taste-wise and nutritionally poor that when we are through dieting, because we have been so *good,* we reward ourselves by eating all the same foods again that we gave up. We don't realize that what we need is to stay away from the refrigerator at night! This critical thing is not merely dieting, but developing a whole new attitude toward food and health.

We should learn not to blow our cool, and to wait for one second before we put our foot in our mouth. Do we really want that person to push our "mad" button? One of the best examples of a person who took one second to think before he acted is this true story.

When I was a Lutheran pastor in Canoga Park, California, a member of the church stopped by my office. Each morning he had coffee with a friend who worked for a ready-mix cement company. That morning his friend was late, and when he finally arrived, his face was white. Ed asked what was wrong. His friend explained that he had filled up his truck with cement and was coming to the coffee shop when he realized he had left his wallet at home. As he approached the house, he saw there was a new black Cadillac parked in his driveway. He quickly walked into his home and saw his wife in bed with another man!

He didn't know what to do. Should he shoot both of them? Or what? He got his wallet and walked out of the house without a sound. Then he backed up the cement mixer to the Cadillac, and rolled up all the windows but one. Into that window he unloaded all of his cement. His biggest worry afterward was how to explain the missing load of cement, but his boss was more than understanding. Can you imagine the look on the "other man's" face when he left the house and found his brand new car full of cement, with buckled wheels. It made a beautiful picture in the evening paper. The truck driver took time to think and what he decided to do had a real touch of class.

The secret of it all is this: if you can learn to wait, then you can live with hope!

2

NO NUTS! JUST PEOPLE

A couple in their late fifties had just been seated for their first interview with me. They explained that they were both ex-alcoholics and they were having problems in their marriage. I asked them how they felt about being there. The husband said in a shaky voice that it didn't bother him at all.

I said, "You seem pretty nervous about being here because you are gripping the arms of the chair so tightly I'm afraid you're going to break them right off. Now just relax, and don't be too uptight about being here. I have a very simple philosophy, and it's simply that I don't allow any nuts around here, just people."

To my amazement, he replied, "Well, I'm a nut."

I countered with, "Who said you were a nut?"

"Fifteen years ago I went to a VA hospital and saw a psychiatrist. He said I was a nut."

Again I countered, "Do you believe everything anyone tells you?"

"I am a nut!"

I thought I was losing, so I said, "Look, there are some basic reasons why I don't allow nuts around here. It's that I only work with people; so for me to relate to you as a person means that you must be responsible for your own change, not me. If you insist on being a nut, then I'll have to admit that you can be a better nut than I can be a nut doctor. That's expensive on your wallet and on my gut lining. Now, I'll ask you again if you want to be people with me."

"No, I'm a nut."

"Well, I'm sorry I can't work with you. Good-by."

This philosophy may be shared by many people. I hope that I am not suggesting that I'm right, and others who treat people differently are wrong. Not at all. After all, each bird whistles through his own beak. All I'm doing with you is sharing how I see people, care about them, and work with them.

I will not take full responsibility for a person's changing his behavior or life. That responsibility lies within the person with the problem. All I can do is serve as a facilitator—a person who will be open, and honest, and caring —and maybe as a role model. After working three years in the drug culture, I developed a high tolerance for failure. But I don't call myself a failure when a person doesn't change. What I do ask of myself is to be there with a person, and to help him try one more time.

To help you understand me better maybe I should share with you how I developed this philosophy. First of all, as corny as it may sound, I love people. I try to accept a person as he is. Now, I'm not going to say that I do it all the time, but I try to understand, without judgment or evaluation, the who that person is. I know that when I had to work in the drug culture, I found out that it did have a profound effect upon me. I had to listen, without prejudgment, to get beyond facades, and masks to hear the real person.

There have also been several other factors which have helped in my professional growth. I thoroughly enjoyed my work in the Lutheran ministry. At the same time the more I worked with my congregation and counseled them, the more I realized I didn't know.

To help my growth I read a great number of books on psychology and attended graduate courses in clinical psychology for the sake of knowledge. What a relief to go to school for knowledge and not for a grade!

I was privileged to study with Eric Berne in his home in San Francisco before he became famous and before he wrote the book—*Games People Play*. At the same time I was very fortunate to study at the Mental Research Institute in Palo Alto, including a course with Virginia Satir in conjoint family therapy.

The whole world of communication theory helped change my life and the way I listened and worked with people. Also during this time I spent one day a week at a state hospital in training as a volunteer group therapist. I had taken group therapy course at Cal-Berkeley prior to that. This had a very powerful influence in my life.

I never will forget the first time I was to conduct a group at Napa State Hospital. In all honesty, I was very nervous about what and how to conduct therapy in the state hospital. To prepare myself, I obtained a list of the people who were assigned to me. I went through the psychiatric records and tried to remember all that was said about each person attending the group therapy. I read psychiatric reports, the psychological testing reports, the social worker's history of the person and the comments of the attendants on the ward. Thus fortified, I was as ready as I could be to meet the people in my first group therapy session.

But to my surprise and amazement, none of the people in the charts showed up for the group. They all had the same names, but they were not the people I had read about. Then it dawned on me that I hadn't learned much about the people in the group. I had only learned a great deal about the people who wrote the reports on the people who had come for group therapy. I learned about the theoretical positions of the psychiatrist, the psychologist and the social worker. I had learned of their perceptions and their views of these people, but I felt that nobody knew the real individuals.

Obviously I could not impress this group by saying that I was Doctor Marvelous—because I wasn't—so I had to tell them the truth; that this was my first group therapy session; that I was not a psychiatrist or psychologist, but a pastor who wanted to learn more about people and group therapy in the state hospital. I also said I was very nervous and unsure of myself, and I guessed the only way I could be in this group was to be myself.

Can you imagine my surprise months later when the head psychiatrist asked me to attend a staff meeting about my group. I began to wonder what I had done wrong! But the psychiatrist asked me, "Why do the people in your groups leave the hospital sooner, and stay away longer than any other group that we are running here on this unit? What's your secret?"

Well, I told him I didn't have any secret. I said, "I'm just myself as a group leader, and I care about the people in the group."

The psychiatrist smiled and said, "That's quite a lot."

One of the concepts discussed in my training, and about which I read a great deal was that the doctor should maintain a therapeutic distance in working with people. Therapeutic distance, I admit, has real safety valves which keep the therapist from getting involved and letting his emotions cloud his perceptions. It can also have a very adverse effect because he can become so cold and detached, so unreal and inhuman, that he loses his value as a therapist.

People who are labeled schizophrenic or crazy try to avoid responsibility for a personal relationship with another person. Maybe the reason they indulge in crazy talk is to let others know that there is really no possibility for a relationship. What they are suffering from is a tremendous breakdown in skills and a lack of desire for honest, open and clean relationships.

Then, paradoxically, what we give them as a role model for change is a person who has been trained to be very cold, detached and uninvolved, with no human empathy and no self-disclosure telling who he is or what he feels or thinks. In essence, what we give them is the very model of their interpersonal problems, a role model of the "schizophrenic." Then we wonder why the sickie doesn't get better!

I have discovered that labels can be very damaging

and destructive to a person, especially if he begins to believe them, and others around him begin to believe them as well. If you were in a mental hospital, knowing it was a mental hospital, being labeled with a term such as a "chronic schizophrenic hebephrenic type" would be enough to put you away for the rest of your life. In other words, it's all right to go to a hospital to have an appendix out, but to have emotional problems is a different story.

Timothy Leary once spoke of labeling people as a "freezing of reality." Once you label a person, you're stuck with it. You never really get beyond that label to find who the person is. We bestow not only psychological and psychiatric labels, but we label by nationality, color and profession. We think that once we have done that we've discovered something about the person. Really what it does is maintain a wall, put distance between us— and it doesn't provide a bridge to a relationship.

Hugh Prather[1] wrote, "Why this need to divide up, classify and neatly package every new acquaintance? For me to try to classify something so complex as an individual human being merely demonstrates my own shallowness. A judgment of another person is an abstraction that adds qualities that are not there, and leaves out what is unique about him. If I classify someone, I turn him into a thing. The only way for me to contact this other person is to experience him and not think about him." Another subtle and insidious danger to labeling people is that we begin to see them (in the field of mental health for instance) as sick people, and so they begin to see themselves as sick people. Who then is really responsible for their "sickness?"

People are taught how to play the blaming game. Blame the world, blame the parents, blame the economy, blame whatever, but don't ever assume personal responsibility for your own life!

Labels also say another thing, that there is a physiological reason for every problem, that behind every twisted thought is a twisted molecule. Very often we are telling people there is no hope by the labels we give and by the way we treat them. I've been thankful that I am a psychologist and not psychiatrist, because I can't give out prescriptions for mind-altering drugs, so that people will not be reinforced by the idea that they have a sickness that can be cured with medicine. I much prefer to have people feel that they can change when they decide what they want to change. Then when they *do* change, they get the credit, not the medication or the great doctor.

One morning a woman in her late thirties walked into my office and said to me, "Am I crazy?"

I had never met her before and she wasn't a member of my parish, so I countered with, "Why would you think that you're crazy?"

"Well, I hear a voice." Now any person who has read science-fiction, or seen a movie or television show *knows* that when somebody hears a voice inside their head, they're crazy!

I wondered if I should hospitalize her and get immediate psychiatric help and medication, but I waited before I rushed to judgment about the voice in her head. I said, "I don't know whether you're crazy or not. What do you think about the voice?"

"Do you think that God is talking to me?" Oh, boy, now there is another one! How many people are in mental hospitals hearing God talk to them, feeling that they are God, or Jesus Christ.

So I said, "I don't know. Tell me what the voice says."

"The voice tells me how to dress, to comb my hair in a certain style, and how to drive my car. When I'm going on a trip to another community, it tells me where to get on the freeway, which lane to stay in and which exit to take off. It really kind of guides me through my days."

I said, "That's very interesting. So far it sounds like this voice has been helpful to you. Could you tell me a little bit about what you have just experienced?"

"Yes, I have just gone through a very traumatic and emotionally disturbing period of my life. I was pregnant with our third child and for some reason my husband became furious with me for being pregnant. He was intolerant toward me, and cruel and mean to me during the whole time. I became very depressed and quit taking care of myself. I gained weight, didn't clean the house, and didn't dress nicely. Then, after the baby was born, things changed and he treated me better. That was when I began to hear this voice, telling me how to comb my hair."

This woman sitting in my office was not overweight. She was trim, very neatly dressed and her hair was styled becomingly.

In appointments that followed, I was able to find out that she had never had very good feelings about herself. And one time I just said "I'll bet you've said to yourself a thousand times or more, 'If I could only comb my hair this way I would be so much happier. If I could only lose some weight I'd feel so much better about myself.'"

She said, "Yes. I have always felt if I could just do those things it would be better." She asked, "Well, do you think that God is speaking to me?"

"I cannot speak for God, but I'm thinking more and more that you are answering your own questions. Things that you have always wanted to do, you are now giving yourself permission to do."

As we continued her counseling for a few more weeks, I still hadn't panicked, put her in the state hospital or put her in a psychiatrist's care under heavy sedation. When she left the office she would get in the car, and the voice would always say "you."

I will never forget the night she came back to the office after she had gotten into the car and said, "The voice said 'I', not 'you'." That was a moment of great joy for both of us because now she knew she didn't need a voice to say "you." She was together enough to say "I will do this, and I can do this, and I can drive. I'm a whole person." I never labeled her, and I learned a lot from that experience, believe me. I learned how to wait.

The philosophy that I have never seen a patient, only a person, makes that person responsible for his own change. If he's not been labeled he can't have a cop-out through a sickness he's not responsible for. I believe as long as we live we can learn behavior if we want to. I'm not saying it's easy, because some of the old patterns and habits have been with us for a long time.

Normally you find people wanting to blame other people for their misery. It would be really shocking to have a couple come in for counseling and the wife say it's her fault the marriage is in trouble because she's a nag; and the husband admit he's a lousy husband and a poor listener!

A psychiatrist friend, Dr. Paul Morentz, once told me

he was awakened at about 2 A.M. from a very deep sleep. He remembered picking up the phone, saying something into it and hanging up. In the morning when he awakened he could not remember what the person had said or what he had responded. He could recall nothing except that he had picked up the phone, said something, put it back down and gone back to sleep. He was concerned and wondered what happened. Later that day the person who had made the phone call came into his office and said, "Dr. Morentz, I can't thank you enough. Last night when I called you your words really saved my life."

Dr. Morentz said, "How is that?" not wanting to admit that he couldn't even remember what he had said.

"When I said to you in a state of panic, 'I'm falling, I'm falling, I'm falling,' you said to me, 'I'm not your parachute. Good night.' It was the jolt in your statement 'I'm not your parachute,' that made me realize if I was going to improve my life and put it together, I'd better assume responsibility for it. And if it fell apart, I would have to assume *that* responsibility also."

I believe that as long as we live we can learn behavior. If we have some bad tapes and some bad habits in our thinking, we can turn them off and change them. If we are afraid to love, we can learn to love. If we are freaked out by fear, we can learn how to be unfreaked by fear. It means that we can change.

One time a young fellow got angry with me because I wanted to take him to group therapy with me, and he wanted to stay and hallucinate. His aberrations were horrible and filled with black magic, sorcery, graves and ghouls worse than anything Hitchcock could conceive. I said, "Look, you're being disturbed by your hallucinations.

Why don't you come with me now and come out of your dream world?"

First he said, "I just want to dream. I just want to stay here. Let me be."

But I just kept bugging him, because I knew he was trying to turn me off by having delusions and by saying I didn't exist in his world. I got him to recognize my reality in the relationship by making him angry. He wasn't going to come with me and he told me where to go. I asked him, "When do you want to quit hallucinating and start living with people?"

A week later on the hospital grounds he came up to me and said, "Doc, you know the week when you were trying to get me to go to group therapy and I was wanting to stay in my hallucinations. You asked me when I wanted to quit hallucinating, and start living in a world of reality. Can we talk about it now?"

And as we talked about it I explained to him that his dream world was his way of hiding from relationships with people. It was his escape valve. He didn't have to choose that route, but could choose another, that of learning how to be close to people. Then he wouldn't need his dreams.

One of the funniest things that happened while I was at Napa was the time we had a group of visiting psychiatrists from the East Coast touring the facilities. One of the visitors was in one of the back wards and became involved in conversation with someone there. The group went off and left him behind. He finished talking and, turning to an attendant, said, "Would you please unlock the door and let me out?"

The attendant said, "Who do you think you are?"

"I'm a psychiatrist, of course."

"Sure you are," the attendant laughed. "I want you to meet Napoleon over here. Now we've got one who's a psychiatrist!"

By this time the doctor began to get very agitated and said, "Now quit joking! I'm on a tour with the group that just left. I really am a psychiatrist!" He became flustered and upset.

"All right now, we are going to have to calm this one down. Better get some thorazine ready for him because he's too disturbed and may become violent!"

No one would listen to the doctor and nobody would believe him. For that brief moment he came to understand what some of the people who have been 'on the couch' feel and experience. He was eventually rescued when the group did a head count before leaving to return to San Francisco. They realized they were missing one famous doctor, retraced their steps and found a very ruffled psychiatrist who learned what it's like to be a patient, when nobody will listen.

One problem in the doctor-patient relationship is that some doctors get carried away with merely being called "doctor." I admit very freely that when I went back to graduate school I wanted that title, too. It's got a great prestigious sound to it! One of my pastor friends, Nick Ristad, who had interned with me many years before, gave me a box of gold stars as a going-away present, so that when I finally got my degree, I could paste them up.

Doctors can get caught up in their own importance and grandiosity and forget that the only water they can walk on is frozen. They don't need to listen to people; people need to listen *to them*. This instant expertise, this whole syndrome of being a doctor, is something that they must watch very carefully, because it's a heavy image to bear, if they're not prepared to bear it.

There is a story about an MD who went to heaven, and in going from this life to heaven, he was able to take along his stethoscope. With the stethoscope around his neck, he appeared at the Pearly Gates and said, "I'm Dr. Jones from earth."

St. Peter said, "That's all right, sir, but you will have to leave the stethoscope here at the gate because you can't wear it in heaven."

"Why not? I'm an important doctor from earth."

"That's one of the reasons. Up here, you see, everyone is pretty much the same. You can't have that stethoscope hanging around your neck, go running around ordering people, and shoving your way to the front of the line for lunch just because you're an important doctor."

"Well!" the doctor grumbled. "I don't think I'm going to like it here."

"I don't think you'll like it at the other place either!"

So the doctor thought a minute—it always helps to think. Then he grudgingly gave his stethoscope to St. Peter, and glumly began his first day in heaven. Lunchtime came, and the long, long food line; and the terrible humiliation of having to stand at the back of the line and wait his turn like everybody else. All of a sudden, along came a man with a stethoscope around his neck, shouting and shoving, ordering and pushing his way through the crowd until he was at the front of the line. He grabbed a tray and went on through first.

This just infuriated the newly arrived doctor, so he rushed back to St. Peter and said, "St. Peter, give me my stethoscope! You lied to me! You lied to me! You said no doctors had stethoscopes here in heaven and that all of us here were the same. Then at lunch today I saw that doctor going through the line. Who was he?"

"Oh, that wasn't a doctor, That was God! Every once in a while he likes to play doctor!"

The need for labels, for status, for masks, and for facades to hide behind are just simply ways of pretending that we are really *something*. Because our secret fear is that if somebody could really understand us, and know our secrets and the skeletons in our closets, they would reject and ridicule us; and *that* would destroy us. Each of us yearns to be accepted. We need to feel that power of approval—not *because* or *when* or *if,* but *as we are*— as human beings. When we can accept ourselves as we are, we can help others to accept themselves.

One of the problems I sometimes encounter in the first interview with a person I have never met before or known anything about is that he will begin to tell me his life story, with all of the details in a very rapid-fire fashion. All of a sudden he becomes frightened by the thought of telling a complete stranger more than he has ever told another human being!

Realizing this, I will sometimes stop and ask him, now that I know his innermost secrets, if it had changed our relationship; if I had condemned him; if I had preached or criticized; if I had done any of these things. He would say no. I tell him I asked those questions because I discovered the hard way that when a person bares his soul too fast, too soon, to me as a stranger, he leaves the office and begins to worry about what I thought of him, so that we never had a chance to feedback. Perhaps the person would never come back in again. If he did come back for therapy, it would be at such a superficial level that it would take weeks, even months, before he could reach that moment of honesty.

What I'm really trying to say is that if we can rid ourselves of some of our labels, our need to impress and our need to hide, and get down to the basic business of being human beings with each other, we'll find that wonderful power of acceptance. How great it feels to have that unconditional acceptance! It's the power to grow, to believe again and to hope for a new day.

3

THE MORE I LISTEN
THE BETTER THEY HEAR ME

Listen to all the conversations of our world
between nations as well as those between
couples. They are, for the most part,
dialogue of the deaf.
Paul Tournier Swiss psychiatrist

Because you can hear doesn't mean that you listen; because you can talk doesn't mean you can communicate. Hearing is an acoustical phenomena that takes place in our ears. Listening is always an interpersonal experience between people. Talking is a sound we make with our mouth and vocal chords. Communication is a dialogue between people. How can I stress the importance of being a listener? The most common complaint that patients have about their dentist and physician is the failure of the doctor to be a good listener. As a professional, many kinds of statistics come to my attention. Surveys have shown that 40 percent of all malpractice suits in dentistry are traceable to a failure in communication during case presentation. Depersonalization of the health care professions is causing a lot of resentment and bitterness because of the fact no one seems to want to take the time to listen. The only reason I'm so pious is because I'm a professional listener. People pay money to have me listen and try to understand what is going on in their life.

One morning, having breakfast in a hotel, I overheard a group of salesmen talking animatedly, with loud laughter, telling one joke after another. Then I was struck by the phenomena that each person was excitedly waiting his turn to try to play one-upmanship with the previous person's joke. With all their talking and loud laughing, I realized no one was really listening. It reminded me of Paul Simon's song *The Sound of Silence.*

> *And in a naked night,*
> *I saw ten thousand people, maybe more.*
> *People talking without speaking*
> *people hearing without listening*
> *people writing songs that voices never shared.*
> *No one dared disturb the sound of silence . . .*

Show me a good listener and I'll show you a kind and warm person; a good mother, a good father and a good lover. Show me a good listener, and I'll show you a winner —someone who has the ability to make people feel that they are for real. If it is so important to be able to hear a person and not just words, why have we failed so miserably in the art of listening. How many of us has ever even taken a course in how to become a good listener? Maybe it should be added to our school curriculum, along with reading, writing and arithmetic.

Nichols and Stevens in their book *Are you Listening*[1] report this experiment on listening behavior. Teachers were instructed to interrupt their classes at random and to ask students what they were thinking about; to ask them what the instructor was talking about and to write it all down. Here are some of the very discouraging statistics:

90 percent of the first grade students were listening

80 percent of the second grade students were listening

43 percent of junior high school students were listening

28 percent of high school students were listening

Based upon a projection of these figures, can you imagine how professional people would rate as listeners, since they have all attended college and graduate school? Frightening, isn't it?

Nichols and Stevens also tell of a Pharaoh who lived in the year 4004 B.C. who was very sensitive to people. He instructed his aides who were assigned to listen to the complaints of his people to remember it was more important for the plaintiff to be heard than to feel that his problem had been solved. Pretty wise for an old Pharaoh!

I think there are two types of listener. One is deliberate and tuned in very carefully to the content of a message. He evaluates, criticizes and judges if the material being presented is good material, and is well presented and worth listening to. The second is more interpersonal or subjective relationship listening. This is trying to hear a person without necessarily criticizing or evaluating what is being said; withholding judgment and trying to understand the underlying interpersonal message.

Let me give you an illustration from my own personal life. My middle son, Danny, was in the fourth or fifth grade, and on days when I was home would always ask me to please help him with his math. Naturally, the subject that interested me least in school was mathematics, and trying to understand modern math was not my biggest thrill. So I spent some time with Danny and tried to read the book up to the point where he was on a problem. We read it over and over and over in our attempt to understand modern math. I would ask him if he finally grasped it, and he would say he didn't and that we should try it one more time.

Then suddenly it began to dawn on me. The nights I was out, I asked my wife Jeannie if Danny asked her for any help with his math. She told me he just worked and got it done. I finally figured out he wasn't asking for help with his math. What he was asking of me was, "Dad, can I spend some time with you?"

I was finally hearing the second level of the message. So the next time he asked me for some help with his math, I said, "Danny, you know I'm not very good in that subject. I have a feeling that you can get through pretty quick all by yourself. Why don't you finish your homework as fast as you can, and then we'll have some time to be together and talk. How does that sound?" You can imagine how quickly his homework was done!

I spend quite a bit of time traveling as a consultant, teaching human communications and the art of listening and practice management. After a conference, people often will hand me special "jewels" which I put in my briefcase, and may not take out and examine until much later. I don't know where or from whom I received this poem. I don't even know its author.

Please Hear What I'm Not Saying

Don't be fooled by me.
Don't be fooled by the face I wear,
For I wear a mask. I wear a thousand masks.
Masks that I'm afraid to take off,
And one of them is me.
Pretending is an art that's second nature with me.
But don't be fooled.
I give you the impression that I'm secure,
That all is sunny and unruffled with me,
Within as well as without.
That confidence is my name and coolness my game
And that I need no one.
But don't believe me.
Please.
My surface may seem smooth, but my surface is
    my mask,
My ever-varying and ever-concealing mask.
Beneath lies no smugness, no complacence.
Beneath dwells the real me in confusion, in fear,
    in aloneness,
But I hide this.
I don't want anybody to know it.
I panic at the thought of my weakness and fear
    being exposed.
That's why I frantically create a mask to hide behind,
A nonchalant, sophisticated facade, to help me
    pretend,
To shield me from the glance that knows.
But such a glance is precisely my salvation. My
    only salvation.
And I know it.
That is if it's followed by acceptance.
It's the only thing that can liberate me from myself,

From my own self-built prison walls,
From the barriers that I so painstakingly erect.
It's the only thing that will assure me of what I
*   can't assure myself,*
That I'm really worth something.
But I don't tell you this.
I'm afraid your glance will not be followed by
*   acceptance and love,*
I'm afraid you'll think less of me, that you'll
*   laugh, and*
Your laugh would wound me.
I'm afraid that deep down I'm not much,
And you will see this and reject me.
So I play my game, my pretending game,
With a facade of assurance without.
So when I'm going through my routine do not
*   be fooled by what I'm saying.*
Please listen carefully and try to hear what I'm
*   not saying,*
What I'd like to be able to say, but can't.
Who am I, you may wonder. I am someone you
*   know very well,*
For I am every man you meet, and every
*   woman you meet.*

Now let me ask you, "Do you want to become a good listener?" You can learn how to be a more effective listener only if you first *decide* to learn how to listen more effectively. You must expend more mental energy and make a conscious effort to break some of the bad habits of ineffective listening. Practice will be needed for you to develop the skills needed in the art of listening.

Have you ever wondered why so many of us have difficulty remembering people's names? It isn't very hard to understand why. We don't remember them because we never, in fact, hear their names in the first place. We are too preoccupied with our own thoughts, feelings and discomfort. Secondly, if we do hear the name, we don't repeat it so we could make use of it and hear it again. Thirdly, we don't spend energy to associate that particular name with something else to give us a clue.

I've got to tell you a little story about a pastor who had a very difficult time remembering names of his parishioners. Someone gave him a hint that he should listen carefully and then try to give some association to the name. There was one very important person in his parish, an elderly, wealthy widow (that made her *very* important!) whose name was Mrs. Humick. After thought, he decided that he would associate Humick with stomach and therefore never forget her name. He was so proud of himself that the next Sunday when he saw her he said, "Good morning, Mrs. Kelly. How are you?"

To become a good listener, one must first become aware of some of the barriers that get in the way. The first and most obvious one is preoccupation with our own thoughts, anxieties, weaknesses and fears. Maybe we are afraid that our inadequacies will be discovered. Then we fear rejection.

I must confess that one of my greatest sins is my ability to go off on great mind trips which I call "creative adventures of the mind." In reality, I get so preoccupied with my own thoughts that very often someone has to set a bomb off at home to wake me up to listen to them. My wife Jeannie has threatened to write an exposé on what it's like to live with a renowned communicator who listens and communicates with other people but whose family finds him hard to reach at times.

The next barrier is assuming you know what a person

already thinks, feels and needs. This often takes place when one person starts a sentence. The other assumes he knows the complete story and finishes the other person's message. The first person is left with the puzzled feeling, "That's funny. I wasn't going to talk about that at all!"

We often assume that with our crystal ball we know all the facts. Let me test your ability to discern if you know all the facts by recording this account:[2]

> On a cold January day, a 43-year-old man was sworn in as chief executive of his country. By his side stood his predecessor, a famous general who 15 years previously had commanded his country's armed forces in a war which resulted in a total defeat of the German nation. The young man was brought up in the Roman Catholic faith. After the ceremony there was a 5-hour parade in his honor, and he stayed up until three A.M. celebrating.

Who is it? The facts in this account are enough to make the average citizen in the United States immediately assume that it was the inauguration of John F. Kennedy. It was, in fact, an account of the installation of Adolf Hitler as Chancellor of Germany.

As I have said earlier in the book, labels are barriers that prevent effective listening, and inhibit communication between people. Labels are just symbols and merely words. When you give a word a personal meaning it takes on a reality and substance for you. Then you are stuck with it. Labels are ear plugs in interpersonal relationships.

It is very difficult to refrain from judging and evaluating another person's message. Our minds go at a much faster pace than we are able to listen, so it is easy to go out on space trips while we are trying to hear, and only catch parts and bits and pieces of what a person is trying to say. It's natural for us to think of a response before the other person has finished his sentence. When we do that we've stopped listening and are answering messages that people aren't sending.

The second level of listening to a message involves being aware, not only of the message, but the context in which the message takes place. The context will have an effect upon the communicative process. The non-verbal messages from the walls, feelings of the room, the color, the life and the dullness all have some effect upon the room and its ability to hear what even the wall has to say. These influences on behavior are often ignored. For a few moments I want you to use your imagination and listen to the messages from these living environments:

You see a slum with trash spilling out on the sidewalk. A child is looking down at the concrete from steps going into an apartment. What do you hear?

You are in a gray, bleak and barren back ward in a state mental hospital with people sitting on benches. Their appearance is heightened by baggy clothes, and there's a smell that is only too common in such a ward. How would you feel in that environment?

The next scene is of a beautiful, royal blue ocean with whitecaps breaking against a sparkling, sandy beach. The beach is outlined by

palm trees and a few fluffy white clouds How do
you feel about that message?

A warm fire is crackling in the fireplace. The
lights are softly lit and outside the picture window is a scene of a quiet snowfall. Soft music
is playing in the background, and you are there
with the person you want to share that environment. What are your feelings now?

People's behavior and the ground rules of communication are influenced by the environment. Many modern
architects and designers are creatively changing and beau-
tifying the living environments of medical and dental
offices, airports, hospitals and various businesses. It's no
surprise for me to hear of how these positive changes
are affecting behavior, and how excited and pleased are
their clients.

To listen with empathy means to hear the person, not
just the words—to try to see the world through his eyes
—to try to get in touch with the uniqueness of that person.

Reuel Howe states in his book *The Miracle of Dialogue*[3]
that communication is accomplished, not when the barriers are wiped away, but when they are accepted as part
of the dialogue. If we can accept hostile-defensive behavior and become flexible, we can learn how to get
beyond the defensiveness to the person behind the wall.
The defense mechanism is a psychological phenomenon
by which a person automatically protects himself against
being hurt or feeling guilty or anxious.

My goal is to help you to understand defensive behavior, to reduce hostility, and to teach you how to prac-

tice listening to people's hidden messages. This is one of the most important skills you can learn, whether as a husband or wife, a boss, in business or any profession. I hope it will help you acquire some techniques and also reduce uptightness and the knots in your stomach.

If you believe you are threatened by a situation or person, you will normally react defensively and so will the other person. This defensiveness reduces the ability to listen; thus communication becomes distorted and there is a lack of trust in the relationship. Maybe it would be good to discuss the ways defensive behavior is achieved.

Strategy No. 1 — To make people more defensive: Always be critical and judgmental of the other person. Be very quick to point out any faults, flaws or errors in his presentation, his looks or what he says. This will guarantee that he will be more guarded, resistive and hostile. Just remember the last time someone did you the courtesy of raking you over the coals, pointing out every flaw in your character, and every mistake in your work. Maybe you are a secretary who has worked hard all day trying to get everything done. Five minutes before quitting time the boss decides that five more letters need to be finished. Then he blows up and criticizes you for being sloppy in your work and not dedicated to your profession! Always being evaluated and criticized is a sure-fire way to make someone feel insecure and react defensively.

Strategy No. 2. When you want to control a relationship and to manipulate a person to do what you want to be accomplished, arrange the conversation so he can't get a word in edgewise. Bombard him with your brilliance,

use fancy words he can't understand so that he will feel
inferior and stupid. Then, bewildered and befuddled, he
will follow your advice. This is also a very excellent
technique to make him react more defensively and cyni-
cally, and become a paranoid listener.

Vance Packard in his book *Hidden Persuaders*[4] describes how people are bombarded with persuasive messages to manipulate their minds, feeling and wills with
a frighteningly subtle effectiveness.

In dealing with people at home or at work, one of
the first ways to break down someone's defensive hostility is to listen to the second level of what he's saying.
What a person believes or expects in a relationship is
usually based on prior experience. Only until he's made
aware that *this* experience will be different will he turn
off some of his negative tapes and preoccupation with the
past and enter into the here and now.

As a consultant, I have often suggested to business,
dental and other professional offices that they develop
a "zinger" notebook. This is simply a notebook that is
kept in a central place, such as the front desk. Every time
somebody gets a hostile zinger he writes it down in the
zinger book. Then at a staff meeting, the zingers for
the week are gone over and written out on a chalk board
to try to find out what the hidden messages are behind
them. Not only will the staff be trained how to listen to
the second level of a message, but the real payoff is that
no one is afraid to receive the zinger, because he knows
what to do with it. This gets to be a little confusing for
the traditional complainer, who loves to let go with one
more zinger, to see someone standing there with a little

smile on his face, not becoming hostile or irked because he just can't wait to write that zinger down in the book.

This is a very powerful way to hang loose in an office. You needn't be hooked on other people's hangups and let their negative behavior ruin your day.

Now that you have some awareness of what might be said to you on the second level, how do you respond to this hostile-defensive message? What usually happens is that somebody gives you a zinger during the day, and at 2 A.M. you wake up with a brilliant answer. I suggest you write down the zinger in the book together with a list of possible responses you could use.

The following procedures may be helpful to reduce hostile-defensive behavior in people:

1. Respond to the obvious. Maybe somebody's nervous, afraid, distrustful or just plain frustrated. Comment on it. Don't go beyond that until you have given them some feedback on their uptightness.

2. Accept the hostile message. This has a really interesting effect because when you react non-defensively, it's very disarming to the uptight one. After accepting the message, give the person some feedback. Let him know you are trying to understand him; to understand his world of reality. It does not mean that you have to agree with that reality, but that you respect his uniqueness. Most important do not immediately begin to explain or cross-examine the hostile-defensive person.

3. Don't be victimized by the explaining syndrome. When somebody confronts you with a mistake or accuses you of something wrong, don't immediately go into a lengthy explanation.

4. Deal with a person honestly. Remember what Abe Lincoln said. "Tell the truth, so you won't have so much to remember."

5. Dare to be open about the who that you are. John Powell in his book *Why Am I Afraid to Tell You Who I Am?*[5] makes this statement: "To reveal myself openly and honestly takes the rawest kind of courage. I can help you to accept and open yourself mostly by accepting and revealing myself to you." Simply, it means for you to be open and honest and say "Yes, I can understand how frustrating it is to be kept waiting, or to buy something and have it break down." I would feel the same way you do.

These five steps sound very easy, don't they? But they can be very difficult because they represent attitudes that must be learned and practiced until they become familiar. When someone is confronted with a defensive-hostile message, the normal reaction is to counterattack with his own hostile-defensive message, to automatically ask why the other person thinks that. The "why" anyone does this is a very defense-evoking question few of us can really answer.

We give reasons for our behavior, but we rarely know the real reason why we behave the way we do, and so we respond with hostility. It's like saying, "O.K., so you hit me with a rock. I'm going to get a bigger rock!" We call that "war."

The art of responsemanship is a learned skill which you can learn if you decide you want to spend the energy. Please remember that responsemanship is a new behavior. Don't discount yourself and say it doesn't sound like you. If you fumble or stumble around in the learning process, remember you're just being trained in new behavior.

The goal is to learn how to respond to hostile-defensive behavior to break down the defensive walls and, with the power of acceptance and understanding, make the other person feel safe. It is tremendously important to let him know that there is someone who will listen, who will even accept hostility and then offer understanding. When you respond to the obvious and accept the zinger, you're demonstrating a very powerful way to build a relationship. The hostile message is sent, and the sender is expecting a hostile message back, but he does not expect acceptance or understanding. When he receives it, this causes him to turn off his negative tapes and begin to think. I have always said when people begin to think there is always hope.

Each of us has a basic need to be accepted as we are, even at our most unloveable times. Acceptance by another frees a person from the prison of the past and allows him to grow and experience a new relationship. When someone has become very angry with me, I first communicate to them with an open body posture. I show them that I am unreserved and unafraid. This is no time to cross your arms tightly across your chest. I let the person unload what's on his mind and tell me all. When he is finished I lean forward and calmly say, "Are you sure there isn't anything more?" This is not the expected response. The other person feels somewhat awkward because I have accepted his hostility and not reacted in a hostile-defensive manner. Remember this psychological factor—hostility is like a boil; it must be drained before there is healing. Behind the negative hurt feeling, once drained, there is the possibility for positive emotions to surface.

Here, again, are five basic rules to follow in breaking down the walls of defensive behavior:

1. Respond to the obvious message.
2. Accept the hostile message. This does not mean agreement.
3. Through feedback let the person know that you are trying to understand.
4. Don't answer the message or offer an explanation of your ideas or procedures at this time.
5. Deal with the person honestly and dare to reveal yourself as a human being who cares.

When you practice responsemanship always consider your reaction to a zinger, by evaluating it on these criteria.

A. If I respond to the zinger in this manner, have I really heard the second level message?

B. Does this response indicate rejection or acceptance? Will it increase more hostile-defensive behavior or will it take a few bricks out of the wall and now begin to build a bridge to a relationship? Am I really demonstrating that I am trying to understand?

Basic Principles in
Understanding Human Communications

As I said before, because a person can talk does not automatically mean he can communicate. In the history of man never have we been so preoccupied and concerned with communication. Every problem between husbands and wives, between different groups or nations seems to evolve from a communication struggle. The very word communication is so much a part of our vocabulary that it's like the weather—everybody talks about it, but no one seems to do much about it. How important is the ability or lack of ability to communicate? Ask a wife, or a marriage counselor or a divorce lawyer.

Reuel Howe says, "Dialogue is to love, what blood is to the body. When the flow of blood stops, the body dies. When dialogue stops, love dies and resentment and hate are born."

Dostoevsky, in his work, *The Brothers Karamazov,*[6] says, "If people around you are spiteful and callous and will not hear you, fall down before them and beg for their forgiveness." For the truth, you see, the blame for them not wanting to hear you, the failure to communicate is in yourself.

The following basic principles of human communication are the results of the work of the people who have been associated with the Mental Research Institute in Palo Alto, such as Gregory Bateson, Don Jackson, Virginia Satir, John Weakland, Jay Haley, Janet Beavin and Paul Watzlawick.[7] I only wish I could say this was my own original material, but I can't. From these people I am very indebted for what I have learned about human communication.

Don Jackson[8] defines communication as ". . . behavior in the widest sense. Words and their non-verbal accompaniment—posture, facial expressions, even silence—all convey messages to another person, and all are subsumed under the term communication."

The first principal about human communication is a

very obvious one. Man is a very communicative animal. In fact, man cannot *not* communicate. We communicate with words and gestures, body posture, vocal tone, and even our silence is a message.

Another principal is that every human communication is a two-level phenomena. The first level, as stated earlier, is called the content of the message or the report. The second level—one with which we are not familiar through knowledge, but from a life point of view—has to do with the relationship aspect of the message. This aspect, if it is a subjective side of the communication, also has a command aspect that tells what to do with the content of the message. It attempts to establish ground rules, or who can say what to whom about what. The person in charge of the relationship establishes the ground rules and basically determines the outcome or goal, unless the other person countermaneuvers and steers in another direction. A classic example of relationship maneuvers is shown in the dialogue at the beginning of the second chapter.

At the beginning of this chapter, I tried to make you more aware of the hidden message, the one at the second level. To become a skilled communicator, one must learn how to respond to second level messages.

This is a generalization, but I have discovered a sexual difference regarding the two levels of communication. Men apparently are more comfortable with the content level, the first level, the logical deductive, reasoning type of message. In fact, if a wife asks her engineer husband, "How much do you love me?" he might pull out a slide rule and say, "This much." Men can disagree heatedly about ideas on the content level and, after they have had an intense discussion, can put their arms around each other and go have a beer.

Women have a more difficult time staying on the content level since they are much more secure in and sensitive to the relationship aspect. When someone disagrees with a woman's ideas, she feels they are disagreeing with her as a person. Her focus is upon the subjective side of the message. This is why it is often a mystery what went wrong between a man and a woman. A man doesn't understand why a woman gets upset because he just disagreed with her.

In a marriage counseling group a very successful business man said to his wife in September, "Do you want to come with me to Las Vegas in November?" Notice this is strictly a simple content message.

The wife answered, "No, I hate Las Vegas."

In October he asked his teenage daughters if they would like to come to Las Vegas in November. They turned him down also, saying that Las Vegas was a drag. A week before he was to go to Las Vegas, he said to his wife, "It would mean a great deal to me to have you sitting in the audience when I give the keynote address at the national convention this week." Did she go to Las Vegas? You better believe it!

Now what was the major difference between the first time and the last time? The first time the message was a rather rhetorical content-oriented message about going to Las Vegas. The final message was about relationships, and how important it would be for this husband to have his wife with him there. That's true relationship talk.

What people need in a work relationship, or a family or marriage relationship, is for people to develop the ability to communicate more on the second level. To talk about how valuable a person is to them and to offer words of praise, of thanks and love are very powerful relationship messages.

I want to comment again about the difficulties males and females sometimes experience in communications. Because men are not skilled in listening to the subjective side of a message, they often get into trouble with women. Because women, it has been rumored, are often very devious communicators, they leave their men completely buffaloed, bewildered and baffled.

As an example, for instance, a wife has been wanting to go out and see a particular movie for some time. Instead of being straight-forward and saying to her husband, "John, would you like to go see a movie on Friday or Saturday night? Which would suit you best?" a hint is given. She says, "It's been a long time since we have been out, hasn't it?"

"Yeah," the husband will say.

"You know, I was talking with Mary the other day at bridge, . . ." (and her husband at this point starts tuning out further and further because this is just more "woman talk") ". . . and she and her husband saw the movie and they liked it a lot."

By this time her husband is not really listening at all. The wife is thinking that maybe he has gotten the hint. She wants him to feel that it is his idea to see the movie on Saturday night. Saturday comes, and no movie! That night the wife is rather moody. Her husband is quite puzzled and can't imagine what went wrong! He tries to become a bit amorous, but she is very cool.

Finally he says, "What's the matter, dear? What did

I do wrong? I thought we had a beautiful day. We played golf and went shopping together. I cooked some nice steaks for dinner. What's wrong?"

"Oh, nothing; nothing at all."

"What do you mean, 'nothing at all?' Why are you so quiet?"

"You wouldn't understand!"

"What do you mean I wouldn't understand?"

"Well, I wanted to . . ."

"You wanted to what?"

"Never mind. You're just impossible!"

"What do you mean I'm impossible? I don't even know what you're talking about."

"That's what I mean. You never listen to me at all."

Then they go to war and have a real breakdown in communication. Because the husband wasn't skilled in how to listen to women, he didn't know that what his wife was verbalizing was not what she was really saying.

Sometime when I meet God, I'm going to ask Her why She made women so complex and difficult to understand! Why do women have such a tendency to overpersonalize a simple statement and get upset about it and pout? Why can't they be more direct in their communication? As Alan Jay Lerner lyricizes in *My Fair Lady,* "Why can't a woman be more like a MAN?"

Before some of you call me a male chauvinist pig, remember I'm just generalizing. These are simply a few rumors I've heard in twenty years of marriage counseling, and twenty-four years of marriage!

Sometimes we also engage in what I call "tricky" or "double-bind" communications where you're damned-if-you-do and damned-if-you-don't. Once in a while Jeannie will ask me, "Do I look a little heavy in this dress?" I used to bite on questions like that, but I've finally learned the hard way! If I say, "No, you look just beautiful, honey," she could say, "You really don't care how I look any more, do you." So I lose there. If I say "Well, come to think of it, you do look a little bulgy in a few places in that dress," I'm criticizing her. I'm in trouble either way! So now, when she sends me a double-bind message, I just honestly say, "No way will I answer that one!" A double-bind message simply means the content says one thing, and the relationship message says, "Ignore the above-said content."

I think I learned one of the trickiest bits of communication one evening when I went to Eric Berne's home in San Francisco for our study club. The group discussed Martian talk, or sending a message in which the contents sound all right. However, they've got a hooker on the side that says, "Go get into trouble."

For instance, you visit a friend's home with your young child and you spot a beautiful porcelain figurine on the coffee table. You are worried about the child playing with it, so you point to it and say, "Don't touch that figurine."

The child walks toward the table and says, "What figurine?"

"Don't touch it!"

"You mean this figurine, mommy?"

"Yes, that figurine. Don't touch it!"

He makes a grab for it and you spank him because he's been bad. Really, what you have done is communicate in Martian. You pointed it out to him and said, "Now go get in trouble!"

I know this has happened frequently. Parents, taking

a child to the dentist for the first time, will say, "I don't think it will hurt too much."

The child will think, "Does that mean I am going to be hurt?"

Or mommy says, "Remember, your mother is just outside."

"You mean I'm going to need rescuing?"

Then a funny thing will often happen which has been verified by many dentists. They will have a young child in for a first appointment, and everything goes just beautifully. The little child is absolutely enchanted. He goes through and looks at the tools and everything in the office, and has a really neat time. Then as he leaves the operatory he sees his mother and remembers that mother said he would be afraid and be hurt, but that she would be there to rescue him. Mother is always right, so now the little guy runs to her and begins to scream and holler. Mother glares at the dentist and the staff for being such cruel monsters. The dental staff is completely astounded, bewildered and puzzled, because they know the child had a very happy experience in the dental chair.

Art Linkletter had a great strategy when a child would not talk on his T.V. show. He would say to the child, "Tell me, what did your mother tell you to be sure not to talk about?" Then the kid would open up and spill the beans all over the place. So I teach the dental staff to ask the child, "What did your mommy or daddy say to you about coming to the dentist for the first time?" This is a very good clue to see how they were programmed and if they were given any Martian talk about being afraid of the dentist because mom and dad are afraid.

After the child responds, they can say, "Well, maybe

mom or dad had some fear when they were children, but you didn't have any pain or fear, did you? Why don't you go out there, put your arms around mommy's neck and say, 'Mommy, it was all right. You don't need to be afraid of the dentist any more.' O.K.?" Children love to go along with it, and they will take care of mom's fear.

Years ago there was a young couple that came in for marital counseling. The problem was that the wife seemed to have the ability to go to bed with different men rather casually and easily. Her husband said, "Why? We seem to get along very well in our marriage. Why are you so casually able to have an affair with another man?"

She came up with an answer something like, "Well, I keep hoping that I can learn some new techniques to make you a better lover." You know how much that builds a man's ego!

I said to her, "Now, wait just a minute. I find that rather hard to believe. Would you please tell me what your mother told you about sex when you were a young girl?"

These were some of the Martian statements her mother gave her:

"Don't ever sit on a boy's lap!" (I can almost hear the little child saying, "I wonder what will happen?")

"Don't ever kiss a boy too long." ("Oh yeah? What then?")

"Don't ever pet too passionately or you won't be able to stop." ("Really?")

Without realizing it, the mother was giving her daughter a very straight message with a Martian hook saying, "Go, get into trouble sexually with men." Until she realized her programming, she could not really change.

Then she was finally able to make a decision about what to do with her mother's Martian injunctions.

Since we communicate in many forms, such as words, messages with a double meaning, body gestures that don't match the verbal message, the tone of voice and the context all have an effect on how a message is received.

Recently I received this plaque after lecturing at a dental convention. It read: "Your visit has climaxed an already dull day." I assure you that this was said in a spirit of good fun, but it does lead us to explore the use of humor as "tricky" communication.

Humor or teasing can be difficult to deal with because there is a fine line between having fun with someone and making fun of someone. If the other objects about the humor hurting his feelings, the teaser can say, "I didn't mean any harm by what I said. Can't you take a little joke?" If it is so harmless, the person being teased wonders, "If no harm was meant, why do I feel a knife sticking between my shoulder blades?"

When Adolph Hitler came to power in Germany, one of the first actions taken by Goebbels was to forbid the publication of political satire in newspapers. He fully understood destructive disqualification through humor. In 1938 when the Nazis captured Sigmund Freud in Austria, they were caught in a dilemma as to what to do with him. They did not want to tip their hand of anti-Semitism at that time, but they couldn't allow Freud to leave Austria without some way to rationalize his leaving. Thus he was asked, in return for an exit visa, to sign a statement that he had been treated with the respect and consideration due his scientific reputation by the German authorities and particularly by the Gestapo. The Nazis wished to use the document as propaganda, but they made the fatal mistake of allowing Freud to add one more sentence. Listen to the content of Freud's statement and realize the double meaning. He wrote, "I can heartily recommend the Gestapo, to anyone." His words of praise were the supreme sarcasm, which made the document useless as propaganda.

In human communications there are basically three types of relationships one can have with other people. We're most familiar with the first one which is the parent-to-child. One person is in charge and defines the ground rules for the relationship, with the other person in the inferior position. Naturally a new baby can't be treated as an adult and equal, because it can't take care of itself. The relationship places the major responsibility upon the person in the one-up position. This type of situation is also experienced in doctor-to-patient, teacher-to-student and boss-to-employee. It is difficult when children are growing for us to be able to shift from the parent-to-child to a more adult-to-adult. Ideally, we want children to assume more responsibility for their lives, and for us to have less and less responsibility.

The next relationship is defined as the adult-to-adult where both parties consider each other as equal and can respect each other's uniqueness. The partners can even have different strengths as in a marriage and different areas of interest. Through their ability to communicate and collaborate, they may share diverse responsibilities, but basically it's an equal partnership. Once in a while you can have competitiveness between adults where people try to play the one-upmanship game.

The third type sounds like the first one, except the

person in charge of the relationship is in the one-down position. For example, the words that send chills up and down my spine is when someone comes in for an appointment and says, "Dr. Olson, I have heard that you are such a great doctor. I will be a terrific patient, believe me —a very cooperative patient." That sounds like they are allowing me to be a doctor. But basically they are in charge of that relationship. They are the ones that are setting up the ground rules. I've got news for you! If it stays that way, and I don't countermaneuver, they can be a better patient than I can ever be a doctor. They can play games and manipulate and frustrate me from a one-down position.

There is an old cliche in communication theory that goes like this: "I know you believe you understand what you think I said, but I'm not sure you realize that what you heard is not what I meant."

To put it another way, when a person sends a message to another person, the message received is not always the message sent. When two people, with personal programming and beliefs about themselves, attempt to communicate with each other, they try to build a bridge between two unique worlds of reality, so that they can overlap and have feedback. Unfortunately too many of us assume that there is only one view of the world—our own view. In my experience, if the responder indicates that he does not perceive the world or receive the message in the same way as intended, the message-sender can be upset and feel that the other person is mean, stupid or crazy.

How important it would be if we would learn to ask for feedback by simply saying, "This is what I heard you

say. Am I hearing you correctly?" Or, "I'm not sure
I understood you on that. Would you repeat the message
again to me?" If we have a correction or feedback, we
have a chance for clarification and understanding. Thus
we know that there is always a built-in potential for
failure to communicate because of the uniqueness of
past experience and the degree of perception in each individual.

Laing, Phillipson and Lee in their work *Interpersonal
Perception*[9] state: "In order for the other's behavior to
become a part of self-experience, self must perceive it. The
very act of perception entails interpretation. The human
being learns how to structure his interpretation through
his experiences in his family and his sub-culture and his
overall world experience."

For instance, if we see a man crying, the behavior is
crying, but it can be experienced and labeled in many
different ways—as being sensitive, as being weak, as
warm, as emotional or depressed.

To experience an event in all cases means that the act
of perception will cause an interpretation of that perception. For many things we see and hear we select only a
few to remember. The same act may be very significant
to one person and very trivial to another. We may not be
paying attention at the same moment someone else is per-
ceiving and we might have missed a very significant ges-
ture or statement. To perceive an event is to interpret it.
In fact you can't help but interpret it . . . For instance, if
I said the word "flower," everyone of you would automatically give that symbol some interpretation, maybe a
rose, maybe bread (if it's close to lunch time), or a
daisy. Whatever it was you would find a way to interpret

it. So much of our communication takes place on the edge of our awareness. Each of us also have words that set off emotional reactions within us because of our past life experience, and these reactions will also cloud and put barriers in the way of a communication relationship.

Now, I would like to spend a little time dealing with some of the ways in which we can develop new ground rules and new ways of talking, so that we don't go to war in our relationships and can enjoy each other much more easily. Again, I will say that you will have to develop some new ways of talking and listening.

One of the most frustrating things in human communication is to have somebody disqualify you, to set you up, either by silence or changing the subject or to mind-read you. It makes you feel that the message you have inside to send to that person is never completed and this leaves you with the frustration of an incomplete transaction. This is where we often fail in our ability to communicate. We keep the frustration there, and let "I don't want to listen to you" be the closer. Instead, I would suggest that you say, "I would like to renegotiate that transaction. I am still very frustrated and when you retreated into silence or changed the subject, I am still left with a problem. I don't want to go to bed tonight feeling this same frustration going on around in my mind. When can we talk, so you can let me at least be heard?"

It is a mystery to me why people so easily accept another person's communication maneuver to end a transaction, even when the process of communication may have just begun. Let me give you some examples of how a person may attempt to frustrate another person by stating, in essence, "This closes the subject."

My mother used to tell me when I was a little boy and she needed to correct me for something I had done wrong, I would say "Let's skip it mom. O.K.? Let's skip it!" My memory is a little hazy as to whether my maneuver to get off the hot seat worked or not, but at least I tried to end the unpleasant conversation.

Here's a familiar scene—a mother has been working out in the yard and her oldest son comes home from school. She says, "Son, will you help me finish cleaning up the back yard so I can start supper?"

The son counters with a message, "Look, mom, I'm beat. I've had a rough day at school, two tests, and I just don't feel like helping you now."

If a mother reacts normally, she will allow this closer by her son to end the transaction, which leaves her with the job of finishing up the back yard, rushing to get dinner ready and being emotionally frustrated and upset for the rest of the evening. Is there another option open to mom? Yes. All she needs to do is not to allow her son's message to be a closer. She could renegotiate the transaction by saying, "Look, son, I know you are tired and don't feel like helping me pick up the yard. But I'm tired too, and I've been busy all day. So I would like you to help me even though you don't feel like it. Besides I still have dinner to fix, so let's get on with it."

A husband and a wife are going out for an evening, dinner and a play that they have both been wanting to see. As they are getting dressed the husband asks, "Honey, do you know where my new cuff links are?"

The wife explodes and says "Look, I'm not your mother. Do I always have to keep track of everything for you? Can't you even get dressed by yourself?"

The husband has two ways to handle this hostile outburst. First he could react very normally, and counterattack by saying, "Look, whoever said I wanted you to be my mother? All I asked was if you knew where my new cuff links were. I had a hard day, and now you spoil the whole evening. What a waste of money! I work myself to death for you and the family, and that's the thanks I get—an old housewife, nagging at me for nothing." The stage is now set for either a bickering war with indigestion and headaches; or for a cold war and sulks. This is a normal reactive way to ruin a beautiful evening.

The other course open to the husband is to wait one second to think, "Do I want to go to war this evening with my wife, or do I want to enjoy a loving time together?" Taking time to think stops him from reacting in a habitual non-thinking, destructive way. He can renegotiate the transaction by saying, "Honey, you came on like super-mom, and I almost blew up in return. But I would like to renegotiate my request. I want us to have a good time tonight since we both haven't been out for a long time. Without pushing your mad button, all I really want is information concerning my cuff links. Let's start over again, only no war this time. O.K.?" Then he can give her a hug and everything feels all right again.

I have a feeling that some of you are thinking, "Ken, people just don't react like you describe on how to renegotiate a transaction." I will agree that most people do not normally talk that way, but that's the problem. People *can* set new ground rules on communication and problem-solving in their relationships. Remember, sometimes all it takes is to wait one second and think before you put your foot in your mouth.

An old communication guideline, still as good today as it was 2,000 years ago, is to not let the sun go down on your anger. This is not easy to do, and we will fail at times, but it's so much finer to end the day at peace with each other than to sulk, and toss and turn all night. I have actually been in the houses where couples had not spoken to each other for weeks. The emotional tension was so great that you could sense the electricity in the air. Then I would ask what the war was all about. They would invariably hem and haw, and finally admit that neither one could remember why they were fighting. Each person's stupid pride was a barrier to ending the war. Is it really that difficult for a person to ask forgiveness and say they're sorry they blew it? In relationship wars, remember, both parties are responsible and guilty for keeping the war going.

When you don't know what to say to someone, and you're anxious as to what reaction your message will evoke, a very effective way of communicating is to simply wonder out loud what you are about to say, and how it will effect the relationship. When do you use the wondering out loud message? Simply any time you wonder what to say to a person. Say it as you wonder. This puts the focus of the message on your problem, and its communication and therefore hooks the curiosity of the other person. Who doesn't like to eavesdrop on someone else's problem? This wondering out loud message is less likely to increase defensiveness on the part of the listener and consequently he will be more open to what you are trying to say.

The next ground rule that I would like to suggest is so obvious and so filled with common sense that one wonders why it is so uncommon. That is to try to speak the truth in love.

It's a very baffling mystery why it is interpersonal relationships when things have gone wrong, or when we are afraid that something will go wrong, we lie, we are deceitful, we are devious, we do anything and everything to try to avoid speaking truthfully to the issue, lovingly. When somebody tries to manipulate you, and your stomach lets you know this person is trying to push a button if you try to play the nice guy, all you are is a nice setup or the pawn in a game. Try speaking the truth but in love.

When two or more people are involved in a relationship that will develop into an ongoing one, there must be a system of ground rules about communications. The whole is more than the sum total of the individual members. The system concept means that whatever happens in this group, there will be a reaction to the action.

For example, a married couple develops its own set of rules about who can make decisions about money, fun, work, intimacy, sex, etc. Very often this system of relationship creates a balancing out, or homeostasis. But it's not hard to imagine the reactions to this balance if the husband comes home one day and his wife informs him that her mother has just moved in with them. The husband may react to this change by saying, "I'm sorry, but your mother either leaves or I do." The husband's reaction is an attempt to restore original balance to their marital relationship.

Before anyone jumps to the conclusion that I have it in for mothers-in-law, let me make a personal statement. I have been blessed with two exceptionally wonderful mothers. As for having a mother-in-law move into your home, I was the one who started the discussions which led to my mother-in-law, whom we affectionately called "Muddy," to move in with us. I think you can believe me now when I say Muddy is a very special person to me as she is to my wife Jeannie, and to our sons and daughter.

Change in a system is like throwing a rock into a pond of water. A person can't say he only wants three ripples, because the ripples will go out until they reach the boundaries of the pond. Change in a system varies as to whether it is closed and brittle, or is open, adaptable and flexible.

One system demands tight control of the persons in it. The other allows for change, for communication as a process, and feedback to correct and grow as an open-ended network. Instead of high control of people, there is trust and flexibility. Change is not so threatening to an open system as it is to a brittle and closed one. Change in an open relationship is only a problem or opportunity to be explored and decisions honestly discussed by the members.

To put it in a nutshell, the basic problem is lack of trust in oneself and others. If people have never trusted you and treat you as if you needed to be controlled, why should you trust them or yourself.

Here is where negative programming is most apparent. Watch out for people. Always look for the worst in others and you'll always find it. People are critical and cynical about you, so why shouldn't you be critical and cynical about them? This results in being defensive, paranoid and fearful. Fear is used to help keep the troops in line. It's very ironic, but true, that what a person believes is often what he receives as a self-fulfilling prophecy.

Jealous marriage partners who have fixed ideas that they cannot trust their spouses cause the innocent partner, by constant nagging and accusations, as much trouble as if he or she had been unfaithful. It is not surprising that because of this lack of trust the wife or husband finds someone else. Then the jealous one feels righteous indignation, knowing the other couldn't be trusted all along.

Leadership styles in this rigid, non-trust system make an interesting but depressing study. The boss can use various strategies to control the workers beneath him. One style is that of confusion. Creating fear and uncertainty about what is to be done makes employees feel like they are walking around on a 45° angle. When the leader finally decides on a new direction or goal, whether it's good or bad, the workers are relieved that they at least know what is to be done.

Another style is that of the benevolent dictator who develops many rules and regulations for his employees. He assumes he always knows what is best for the company. Therefore, he doesn't need to listen to other people's ideas, but they need to follow his ideas and procedures. There is a great stress on form, and doing things the "company way." Now he may come up with some good ideas, like being nice to people by remembering their birthdays with a card, having company dinners to prove they are all one big, happy family.

Quotas and gimmicks are used to motivate the employees. The leader is always looking for a new strategy to spur on the employees. There is no open communication system, but pockets of people who whisper at lunch or coffee breaks.

The result of this kind of management is a dependency upon the leader, subservient yes-men, passive-aggressive behaviors evident very much of the time in time-off for sickness, high job turnover, apathy and just enough production to keep a job. A system of fear and control produces an immobilizing effect of fear and distrust.

School systems are most often run in this same style of management. This example is a little exaggerated to help make a few points. The school board remembers that it was elected by the taxpayers to help run the school system—but it's soon apparent that most taxpayers don't trust the school board members. After all, what kind of a person would want that kind of a job? There must be something in it for him as a school board member.

The school board hires a new superintendent, preferrably someone from out of town so that he won't already be familiar with the problems. He must be bright and willing to play the game; but not *too* bright, so he can be kept in line.

Now, the new hero comes to town, and he hires assistant superintendents that are bright; but not *too* bright so that he can control them and keep them in line. Next, supervisors and principals are looked over to see who will make waves and who will play it safe. This is how a paranoid system is developed.

Now comes a bright, enthusiastic young teacher who is filled with idealism and new ideas to use in the classrooms. She is thrilled with finally having the opportunity to work with children. Soon the class is involved in developing ideas about how to solve the energy problem. Their excited voices concern the principal (after all, we must have quiet classrooms!) so he calls the supervisor to check what is going on in the new teacher's classroom. She certainly must not be following the curriculum guides. The student's voices are happy!

Enter now the supervisor of the curriculum and, to her horror, the class is not following the rules. The new teacher is reprimanded for not building a unit on the grocery store which is what the curriculum guide demands, but the young teacher says the children were not interested in a grocery store. They know all about them, so she asked them what they would be interested in. They got really excited about new sources of energy.

The supervisor responds, "I don't care what the children want! Follow the curriculum guide." And then the veiled threat, "You're new here aren't you! It will be quite a few years before you can reach tenure." So the school system works to produce mediocrity and boredom because of the control of fear.

Across our nation many schools are in trouble. The inability to be able to discipline the rowdy and sometimes violent student is critical. Teachers have reported an attitude of "Why try?" and of emotional apathy to their profession. After all, what good is it to send a student to the principal's office for discipline if nothing happens and the destructive youngster just returns to the class and sneers at the teacher? Teachers feel a lack of support from

administrators and parents. It's a tragic commentary on
our society, when armed guards and policemen have to
ride school buses and patrol highways and bathrooms.

If situations such as this exist in your community, you
can sit back and complain and say, "It ain't fair," and
"Ain't it awful!" Or you can get involved and put some
backbone into the school system. Find strong principals
and then back them and the teachers. Hoodlums don't
belong in public schools to tyrannize children, teachers
and administrators. The only language a hard-core person
understands is strength and discipline.

I also feel that busing is bad for children. My point is
not anti-racial integration, but simply that it is bad because
it disrupts a child's day by making it too long. The children rise early to catch a bus that takes them out of
their neighborhood, and then return home late usually
with no playtime. They need to have time to develop
friendships where they live, to play and to do nothing.

Have we ever considered how much time children
from the age of five spend away from home in the environment of school? Or what happens in schools when
teachers and peers exert a powerful influence in the psychological growth or psychological defeat of children?

Rigid and brittle systems of relationship, with the psychological climate of low trust and the need for controlling people, is by no means isolated in the school
system. In businesses, professions—wherever people work
together—this philosophy is experienced to one degree
or another. If we don't believe in the people who work
with us, then they react defensively, and work suffers and
becomes only a job.

Robert Townsend, author of *Up the Organization*,[10]

tells this story. Once upon a time there was a small department in a large organization—a typical pyramid: a vice-president, below him a manager, a secretary and five workers. To mesh with the rest of the company, their work had to be errorless and finished by 7 P.M. It wasn't. Here is what was going on. The workers would take their work to the manager who would make a few changes; otherwise why was he there? He would send it to the vice-president who would make a few changes. Why? What else was he there for? The troops had learned that whatever they did they would have to do it over, so they were giving the job a lick and a promise with the work finished at 11 P.M. and full of errors.

For once the traditional error of adding more bodies was avoided. Instead, the vice-president, manager, and secretary were de-hired. The workers were called together and told how much was available for wages and salaries. They were to consider themselves a partnership and hire whomever they needed. Pay would be whatever the budget would stand. But they were to get the work done, without errors, by 7 P.M.

For a while the work suffered, but one day things began to come together. The partners did not need anybody else so they were able to raise their salaries 20%. They split up the responsibilities and discovered to their amazement that they could come in at 10 A.M. and still get the work done without errors by 4 P.M. They were all having a ball. The rest of the organization was jealous as hell. The point is five people in a partnership work a lot better than eight in a pyramid. Fewer people, paid more, tend to produce excellence at no overall cost except to the people who got fired.

An open participative type of organization is not dependent personalities who have never been trusted in their lives; the kind that wait to be told what to do and then do as little as possible. It is for people who still have a curiosity and a zest for life, and who are willing to participate in problem solving and who are idea factories. The secret of motivation for people at work is the awareness that their ideas, their views and efforts can fully be expressed because they, as human beings, are valued. An atmosphere of trust and the feeling that we care about each other frees a person to expand his abilities and develop his talents. He becomes more productive because the inhibitor, fear, is gone.

Praise is also used for encouragement. Mark Twain once said, "I can live for two months on a compliment." I feel that's too long a time interval for praise, however. Thus, a participative open communications system reduces defensiveness and fear so that workers can concentrate on taking good care of the customers. In the people business, remember that if clients are well taken care of, the company is sure to make money.

Maybe by this time you are thinking it's a miracle we communicate as well as we do! The miracle of communications happen when we become good listeners who can listen at two levels; and not only try to hear what the other person is saying, but also what he would *like* to say.

Relationships grow when people communicate more on the second level, freely love, forgive, and say, "Thanks for being you!"

Bridges to relationships are built when we take the bricks out of the walls of our defensiveness and use them to span the gulf that separates our unique personal realities.

Relationship wars are avoided when someone takes one second to wait and think instead of merely reacting.

Systems of relationships that are open and based upon trust can cope with disappointment, failures, heartaches, tragedies and problems because love is building bridges, not walls.

WHAT DO THE SYMPTOMS SAY?

I have found that one of the quickest shortcuts in therapy is to study the possible message and clue from a person's symptom. I have a large number of co-workers in the field of mental health who would disagree with me because I examine the symptom and I may never find the underlying cause. They feel if I don't find the underlying reason for the symptom it will pop up again someplace else.

If a person no longer has the symptom that caused him to seek help, it does not necessarily mean that there will never be any more problems in his life. I think that symptoms are learned and often serve a purpose and in fact are a means of communication if only we can decode the message.

Symptoms can also be viewed at times as a strategy to control a relationship. A wife who is fearful of meeting new situations and new people can covertly control the marital relationship by developing headaches or diarrhea before going out for the evening. The husband can be frustrated, but his wife has no control over her symptoms. They just happen to her, and she is really miserable about them.

One time I invited a couple to join a marital therapy group. The wife, who had resorted to the "Poor Me" ploy, said, "I can't go into that group because I cry too easily in front of people. Her tape was, "What if I cry in public? Wouldn't that be awful?"

So instead of being controlled by her symptomatic behavior, I gave her this instruction. "Since you cry easily in public, I think it would be best if I announced to the group that this is what you do. Then I'll ask you to cry and get it over with, so you won't have to worry about crying after that."

The woman was shocked and protested my suggestion. In fact, she became angry with me for wanting to place her in such an embarrassing situation, but I told her that if she wanted to work on her marriage, this was the way.

The months went by and she never did cry in the group. She just kept waiting for me to ask her to cry. This made her mad, and she was determined not to obey my command. When I accepted her symptom and then prescribed for it, I was in charge of our relationship.

Years ago when I was a Lutheran pastor in California, I received a phone call from our family physician asking if I would make a hospital call on one of his patients who belonged to our church. I asked him what the problem was. He said he had done all sorts of tests on Sally and all were negative. He had also consulted with a psychiatrist about the case, and he didn't know either.

"Well, what does Sally say?" I asked.

"That's the problem, Ken. She was found asleep in a chair at home and the family, thinking she had fallen asleep watching TV, just let her sleep. When they came home that afternoon and she was still asleep in the chair, they called me. I hospitalized her, but so far as I'm concerned there is no neurological basis for her to be in a comatose state."

I admit I was baffled. I couldn't imagine what was wrong with Sally or what the doctor thought I could do, but as her pastor I went to the hospital to visit her. There was a nurse in the room with her and she appeared to be in a very deep sleep. As I sat by her bed I wondered what she was trying to say by retreating from reality.

I began to recall a series of stressful events that had happened to Sally. Early in the summer she had taken a fall by her pool and had broken her ankle in a very bad place. It was a break that was slow to heal because of an inadequate blood supply.

During the time she was hobbling around, one of her teenagers by her first marriage had been in an automobile accident and this shook her up quite a bit. It was also a very hot summer in the San Fernando Valley and she was most uncomfortable having a leg in a cast and trying to scratch an itch she couldn't reach.

Then the crowning blow came the day the cast came off when the phone rang and Sally, turning quickly to answer it, rebroke her ankle.

Now it was a week later and I was sitting by her bed in the hospital and she was in another world. Not being able to think of anything else to do, I started to talk to her. I'm sure the nurse thought I was some kind of a nut, dressed in my clerical garb, talking to somebody in a coma.

I told Sally I could understand why she felt that life was too much for her, and I recounted all the frustrations she had encountered in going through a long healing process. I finally said, "There's got to be an end sometime, Sally, and I think it's about time you began to come back to your world." As the nurse looked rather strangely at me, I had the courage to say, "You can awaken when I leave the room and you will be all right." I didn't know if this would work, but I thought I'd try.

As soon as I left the room she woke up and appeared to be all right. Her physician was quite pleased, and I was really gratified, though still a little bit puzzled.

Life returned to normal for Sally until one day about a month later when I got a phone call from a member of the family who told me she'd been asleep for four days. When I asked what happened, I was told that her husband had calmly made an appointment to meet her down at his attorney's office and, without any warning, had served her with divorce papers. That night she went to sleep and didn't wake up.

This time she was really out of it and nothing would rouse her. Finally we admitted her to the county psychiatric hospital, since I knew if anything would shake her back into reality, that place would!

About a day later, I got a very frantic phone call from an angry woman—Sally. I got in my car and drove down to the hospital. She said, "You're the one that put me in here, aren't you?"

I said, "Yes, I tried to wake you up but you wouldn't listen to me. You are going to end up back here every time

you go into one of your trances. Don't you dare forget
what it's like to be in the 'snake pit'! Now when I tell you
to wake up next time, you had better wake up."

The reason that she was so upset was that they had
signed commitment papers for her to be transferred that
day to Camarillo State Hospital as a nut. I asked how
long the psychiatrist had talked to her and she said he
had interviewed her for five minutes at most, before de-
ciding to send her to Camarillo. I definitely knew she
wasn't crazy, and asked for another opinion. Another
psychiatrist was called in, examined her and agreed that
she should be released and go home again. Without having
her stop to change clothing, Sally and I went flying down
the Hollywood-Ventura Freeway. It was fortunate we
weren't flagged down by some zealous policeman who
would have certainly wondered about a man dressed in
clerical garb and a woman in a nightgown and robe!

Sally did pretty well for about another month. Then
about 2 A.M. a friend called frantically and said, "Pastor
Ken, Sally's hysterical! This second divorce has really hit
her hard. I hate to bother you at this hour, but would
you please come over?" I wrote down the address, and
when I arrived the woman who let me in said, "Thank
you so much for coming. I think everything is going to
be all right now. I finally got her to go to sleep."

"You've got her to what?"

"I finally got her to sleep."

Then I began to be nervous! There goes Sally into outer
space!

That night as she seemed to be going deeper and deeper
into another world, I said, "Sally, I think you had better
open up your eyes. This is Pastor Ken. Remember when

you got so mad at me for putting you in the hospital
and what it was like to wake up down there? I warned you
then if you refused to listen to me you would end up right
back at county hospital. Don't forget they were ready to
send you to Camarillo. Now I think it is time for you to
come back and to open your eyes." She strained and
strained and strained (have you ever watched a person
try to open their eyes?). "Now open your eyes and stay
wide awake. Don't ever do this again!"

She opened her eyes that night and from the shock
and trauma that had happened to her was finally able to
get back on her feet emotionally. She was a very bright,
intelligent and capable woman, and obtained a job in a
high level executive position. Even though the divorce was
traumatic, she was stronger now in many ways than she
had been in years. This was one of the first times I ever
used the strategy of listening to the symptom and trying
to figure out what the message was and what purpose it
was serving.

I take a "whole-istic" view of man! I do not separate
man—mind and body or soul and body. I believe that
all we are is the whole person. When somebody says,
"It's all in your head," the pain may be very real. Very
often people will be confused by going from one doctor
to another who tells them it's all psychosomatic. He will
fail to follow through and do a very thorough exam. I
have found that the mind works in strange ways to communicate its message. Sometimes if we find the message
we'll find the key.

My main message is to not prejudge a person, give them
a label and put them in a place where they have very little
hope. I admit that there have been times in my practice

that people have come to me with very severe problems, and I have been tempted to follow the normal psychiatric diagnostic categories.

One time a teenage girl, about sixteen, was referred to me by her family physician. He became concerned when she quit eating and had lost sixty pounds. She was pathetic, thin and frightened. I asked her how she felt about being here and to tell me a little bit about what had happened in her life.

She said that last spring she had smoked one marijuana cigarette. And somehow, just from smoking that one cigarette, she believed she was poisoned, and that everything she ate was poisoned, and that she was poisoning the people around her. This sounds like I should have turned her over to the state hospital at that point. But I've learned a little patience before I make a judgment. Then I asked her if she would like to change and think about eating again. She said she just couldn't.

As I customarily do, I asked her what other experiences or changes occurred in her life during the past year. It is amazing how many traumas and shocks can happen to a person and he never realizes the importance of how those events can break him down. It seemed that the precipitating event for her problem was the smoking of the marijuana, but her reaction to it was extreme. I asked her what other painful thing she had experienced recently.

As she hung her head, she tearfully told me she had discovered that her older sister, with whom she was very close, was a lesbian. She had had no previous indication of it, because her sister was nineteen and living away from home. Her sister had no desire to change her life, and the situation was tearing the younger girl apart.

I was beginning to piece together some of the message. I said, "Sometimes we can have symptoms that are a message to another person. I am wondering if the purpose of your not eating is an indirect way of communicating with your sister whom you love very dearly. You resent another girl taking her away from you. Isn't it a way for you to tell your sister 'Look what you are doing! You are killing me! The thought of you being a lesbian and living that kind of life is destroying me!' " Her eyes began to pick up a little glimmer, as if I was on the right path. "Maybe your being very sick is a way of asking her to come back and rescue you; to give up this other way of life!"

It was as if a great burden was being lifted from her shoulders, and she began to identify with this type of thinking. The mind doesn't react consciously but works in a very devious way to communicate its message. The most powerful thing she could do was to show that her sister's behavior was literally destroying her.

Toward the end of the hour, I suggested that, knowing her sister couldn't hear the message and how much it hurt, maybe she could say it directly to her. However she should realize also that her sister had the right to choose her own life, even if she didn't approve of it. Then I asked if she could begin to eat.

She said, "I think I can."

She came back the next week with a big smile on her face and told me she had gained back eight pounds. I began to see her regularly. She began to build more confidence in herself, was gaining back her weight and was doing well in school.

The thing that haunted me was that it would have been so easy for me to leap to a wrong conclusion in this particular case. This girl had given me some classic symptoms which could have led me to believe she was suffering from a severe psychiatric illness called anorexia nervosa. This would call for immediate hospitalization for an evaluation of her condition, and possible commitment to the state hospital. If I had merely reacted to her symptoms and not looked for the underlying cause, I might have closed the door of hope for her life for a long, long time.

Her way of saying thanks to me was to make a wooden cross with rocks glued all over the wood. It is a most prized possession in our library.

The Problem of Pain as a Symptom

Thanks to the media of printed and spoken word, we in this country are hyper-aware and concerned with pain. In fact the phenomena of "pain" itself is now a lively subject of research. It appears we don't know as much about pain as we thought we did.

The fear of pain has filled the physician's office with too many people seeking some magic medicine that is written on a piece of paper with strange markings. I believe we have trained people to demand instant relief from pain. In fact, if a physician doesn't give a prescription he is not considered a good doctor. Patients resent being told that their pain is psychosomatic, or just "in their head."

Instead of telling a person his pain is psychosomatic, which offers no solution, maybe it would be better if the person in pain could stop and think for a minute about what the pain is trying to tell him about his body and emotional life. Is the pain the result of a person abusing his body with too much stress, poor nutrition, poor sleeping habits, excessive eating, consuming too much alcohol, boredom, or allowing negative tapes to do their destructive work emotionally as well as physically? Before a person rushes to numb the pain with a pill, maybe he should listen to what it's saying.

The mind is selective in that it will choose one certain spot of our body to attack, and there is usually a logical reason why anxiety will latch onto a particular area of our anatomy.

Years ago, a physician friend of mine referred a young woman to me who had been complaining of chest pains. She was convinced that she was going to die of a heart attack soon, at twenty-eight years of age. She was in top physical condition and a very healthy young woman because she had been a professional ice skater. Her physician said he had run every possible test on her to check out her heart and could find nothing organically wrong.

He had her placed under observation in a psychiatric hospital thinking that there they might discover the psychological or psychiatric reasons for her complaint. They also could find nothing wrong. They had even sent her out of the state to be screened in another clinic, with the reports all coming back negative.

In our conversations I asked what seemed to trigger this concern and anxiety about her heart. She told me that she and one of her good friends, who was about forty-three, were comparing chest pains a couple of months ago. Only a week later, he died from a coronary. After that, her fear and pain intensified.

Among other things, she finally told me some significant facts. "We lived in upper Michigan. The winters can be very long and very cold there, and my father solved the problem of winter with his own kind of anti-freeze—alcohol. Unfortunately when he drank too much he became very brutal and mean. He shouldn't have been drinking at all because he had chronic heart problems. I hated him very much, I must admit, but I don't feel any guilt about it at all. He was a very despicable man. He finally died of a massive coronary."

"How did you feel?"

"I felt nothing when he died, except maybe a sense of relief. By that time I was skating professionally in an ice show. That was one way to leave home."

"Let me ask you something else. Did your mother ever remarry?"

"Yes, she did. She married a physician."

"Did he specialize and, if so, in what?"

"He's an internist, specializing in the heart."

"O.K., there's another reason why the heart would be selected as the focus for the conflicts in your life. Now tell me how your marriage is going."

"It's been terrible, because my husband and I can't communicate. He closes me out of his world."

"I think you are literally dying of a broken heart."

She began to understand the reason why her mind should select her heart to express the pain in her life. In the couple of weeks that followed I talked with her husband too, and tried to get them to communicate more effectively.

I saw the wife alone, but then there was something that didn't seem quite right. One thing about being a professional performer like an ice skater, you can develop a professional smile. I noticed that she always seemed to have the same smile, even when talking about very sad and traumatic things. I'm known to be very blunt and direct, so I said to her "Patty, will you please wipe that professional smile off your face and tell me about the pain and the hurt that's deep in your heart!"

She said, "The truth is I have been married two other times. The first time I married was to get out of my home. My husband was immature and I was immature and it didn't last long. Then I married somebody I met while I was ice skating. He turned out to be an alcoholic just like my father, only a sadistic alcoholic. I made up my mind that no matter how many times he beat me and slapped me around, he would never see me cry."

"Patty, you have locked up this pain all these years in your heart, right?"

"Yes, so no one would ever know how deeply I was hurt."

"I think the pain is there because you have held all those tears in so long. I'm now going to give you permission to cry for all the times you have been hurt, and all the times you have bitten the bullet and said 'Nobody will make me cry.' "

As one tear after another rolled down her cheeks, she said, "You just can't give me permission to cry like that."

"I just did. I don't want you to think about it, but to really feel the relief that comes from finally letting all the tears from your broken heart come out."

She said "I'm not going to cry. You can't make me cry," as she reached for the box of Kleenex. She cried that day and that night because of all the pain that was released.

You see, there is real power when you begin to listen to the symptoms and their message. Listen to your own body sometime when you are having pain in your head, or your chest, or your stomach. Ask yourself what your body is trying to say to you. Examine the situations. If there is a message that needs to be verbalized, why are you taking it out on your body? This is what people do. They are usually afraid to speak out, so they express it in physical symptoms. Stop and think. What's chewing you up? What is making you so uptight? Your body is trying to tell you something! Tune in and listen! Then there is hope that you can decide to change and be free.

Families and Youth

A young person was sitting in my office, in trouble with school, recently arrested by the police, in turmoil at home. And I asked myself, "What do the symptoms tell me about this person? What message is there in his erratic behavior?"

I know we live in complex times, and in troubled times we have troubled youth. We must not rationalize by thinking that "kids will be kids." Never before have young people been in such deep trouble with drugs and, especially, alcohol. In some states venereal diseases among teenagers has reached epidemic proportions. Have you ever talked to a young teenage girl who has just gone through an abortion clinic where each waits their turn in line? Crimes of violence, armed robbery and burglary are increasing rapidly among teenagers.

There are new school phobias. Children are afraid to go to school for fear of being knifed, shot, beaten up or robbed. Some are so frightened that they will not go to the bathroom because they may be ganged-up on.

Runaways today are different from the searching flower children of the early 60s. As I talked with many of them I sensed their hopelessness, their helplessness and the despair of their own life, as if it had no value. They felt nobody really wanted them and they had no place to go; they were excess baggage at home. To look into their eyes was to see a deep sadness and pain that had been inflicted in their lives.

As a consultant to a girl's home I was overwhelmed to realize that out of just eighteen girls how many of them had known a family member who had been murdered or who had committed murder. Some had even been called into a bedroom just as a parent pulled a trigger and blew his brains out. Not only had they witnessed violence, but they had also been victims of cruel beatings and rapes by the time they were sweet sixteen.

How do you remove this emotional scar tissue and reach them so they can begin to trust and believe again, much less live with hope. Are not these symptoms a warning light that something is seriously wrong in our collective lives as a nation? "Destroy the family unit, and you destroy the nation!" That's nothing new to hear. It's as old as the history of the rise and fall of great civilizations. It's even difficult to define what a family is. The old picture of a family, with a husband and wife and children living happily ever after in their dream home, complete with a white picket fence, doesn't quite seem adequate today.

It would be more accurate to describe a variety of family systems, and then to look at the various people who make up the parts of that system. The authoritarian family system and the over-permissive family system, ironically, have one thing in common—they both can produce children who have similar problems.

The authoritarian system is a hotbed for teenage conflict and rebellion concerning the basic issues of control and freedom from control.

The permissive family system produces a floundering, acting-out child who is trying to get his parents' attention to see if they care enough to say no and stick to it.

The fractured family system is where one parent struggles to support the family, to fulfill the father-mother role and keep the family together. The mobility factor of our population often means that there are no grandparents or relatives close by to help in the nurturing of children. Thus baby sitters, day nurseries and day camps become extended family members.

The collapsed family system is where the family has disintegrated to the point that no one cares for anyone but himself. Self-survival is the prime need. Here the extended family members may be caseworkers from the welfare agency. It takes no great imagination to see that this is an emotionally and physically deprived existence.

There are a majority of other family systems, where there is a healthy concept of caring. This family unit is our hope. I've noticed a trend among young men and women today to delay marriage until they are more settled and are more sure of their own direction in life. They seem to realize how much it takes to make a marriage work in commitment as well as maturity. They are aware that you can't live on an emotional thing called "love." They are also willing to wait before they begin a family.

One of the most important trends in the field of mental

health is a realization of the need to view an individual
in relationship to his family members. This has brought
about an approach called "family therapy." This is where
the family is the unit with problems, and it is treated as a
unit. I've always been puzzled that one child seems to be
singled out as the scapegoat of the family. It's no small
surprise that my doctoral dissertation was "An Investigation of Scapegoating, Favoritism and Self-Blame in
Families."[1]

The scapegoating process appears to be as old as mankind. In the *Golden Bough*,[2] Frazier records numerous
instances in history of public scapegoats, human and other.
He defined scapegoating as a process in which evil influences were embodied in a visible form or material
medium which acted as a vehicle to draw those evils off
the people and the village or town. Through sacrifice or
expulsion of the scapegoat the people were saved. For the
ancient Hebrews the Day of Atonement was climaxed by
the High Priest symbolically placing the sins of the people
on a goat, and the goat being led away into the wilder-
ness, bearing the iniquities of the people.

The same phenomena occurs in families where the
unit seems to stabilize and ward off emotional turmoil by
placing the blame on a family scapegoat. Often a child
senses the emotional conflict between his parents and
tries to be the "cement" in their marriage, or to distract
them from fighting with each other by diversionary tactics.

In a psychodrama one day, a teenager was showing two
other boys how to act out a typical family fight. In the
psychodrama the fight went very well and, at its most
intense moment, I quickly asked the boy, "What would
you do now if you were at home?"

He replied, "Oh, I would run out of the house and throw a rock through the neighbor's window, or I'd bang on the family car with a bat."

"Then what would happen?" I asked.

"Well," he replied. "My parents would have to come out and stop me."

"So when you got in trouble, it stopped them from fighting with each other? Because then they had to stop your destructive behavior?"

Thus when a person is in trouble in school, or with the law or his family, it would be an excellent idea to stop and ask what the message is in the young person's behavior. Is he serving the role of a scapegoat to keep mom and dad from fighting or going crazy? Is he, by his behavior, asking help for himself and his family? If a family needs a scapegoat to survive, then family therapy is about the only way a child has a chance to survive in that family.

Today, other powerful influences bear on a young person's life, such as peer group pressures. The drug culture is drastic evidence of the power of a peer group to change a young person's beliefs, values and behavior.

A child spends many hours, weeks, months and years in school. Be sure, as a parent, to investigate what's going on in school that can make life miserable for your child. Sometimes school is bad for children. It doesn't do his self-concept much value to be labeled, ridiculed, and pressured based upon the philosophy in which failure is a vital element. Troubled young people are mirrors of family life and society values and serve as warning signals about the future stability of a community and a nation. Listen to the symptoms. What are the messages?

One of the most inconsistent answers to help solve these problems has been government grants to start mental health clinics, drug treatment centers, day care centers, and supplemental food for school children. But the first cutback in government spending when things get a little bit tight are the funds for helping children.

I'm wondering if it isn't time for religious organizations to put their faith in action by setting up residential treatment centers, halfway houses, and day care centers. If I were to be critical of the Christian church, it would be that too much emphasis has been placed upon money. Its members have been asked for large amounts to support the church, and too little of this money is given to serve people who are hurting and in need of this redemptive love and caring. I believe that at the heart of our ills is a moral and spiritual problem, and until we begin to emphasize this we are only doing half a job. I wish our churches and synagogues would listen to the children and start caring for the youth. A friend of mine once said, "I came not to be served, but to serve." If religious organizations started caring and serving the needs of the poor, the hungry, the imprisoned, the lonely, the old and the sick it would make organized religion more relevant again. Then there would be hope.

5

POWER OF A FIXED IDEA

*"The more faithfully you listen to the voice
within you, the better you will hear what
is sounding outside."*
Dag Hammarskjold

Have you ever had someone confront you with the very
blunt and direct question; "Why did you do that?" The
why to our behavior is a very hard question to answer.
It's hard for several reasons. When someone asks us why
we did something, we immediately react defensively, and
we look for some way to get off the hook. We can come
up with many reasons, but often I find that in conversation he reveals his fixed ideas and beliefs about himself
and other people. I listen very carefully for the inner
revelations he utters in a matter-of-fact way. Sometimes it
is just an aside. I'll give a few examples of what people
have said, revealing their inner beliefs; ideas fixed in their
minds which are roadblocks in their lives.

Slim was in a psychiatric hospital because he tried several times to commit suicide. I was not his therapist because I was his friend. According to his wife, he was not making any progress, so I asked her permission to visit him, after clearing it with his psychiatrist. During the course of my visit I asked him if he wanted to change his life and if he wanted to be O.K.

He replied, "I don't know."

I said, "What do you mean, you don't know if you want to feel better?"

Then he added, "I think I've done too much damage to my mind already to make it back to life again."

"Thank you. That's what I was looking for."

"You were looking for what?"

"That fixed idea, that you have done too much damage already to your mind that you can't get better. Let me explain," I said. "When I asked you 'Do you want to be well again?' you answered that you didn't think you could ever be well because you'd done too much damage already. As long as you believe that idea, all the time you spend in this hospital, all the medication you take, or all the therapy is only buying you a little time until you kill yourself. You'll kill yourself, not for the reasons that you think, but because of the power you have granted the fixed idea that you've done too much damage to your mind to make it back."

He paused for a moment, and then said, "What can I do to get rid of that fixed idea?"

"First of all, respect the power of that idea and belief. And when it flashes into your conscious mind, challenge it by telling it to get lost; that you're going to push the 'off' button on that tape. Find the words to counter that idea because only then, can you begin to break up its destructive power. Do not push it aside, and don't ignore it." Then as I talked to him about learning how to wait, I said, "Right now the road back may seem too long, but if you can attack that fixed idea, wait for healing and have hope for one more hour, a day and then a week, you will diffuse the power of this fixed idea." He began to realize that he had given up on himself, and he had given up on life. And as long as he had given up, there was no hope.

It has been several years since that visit in the hospital. He is doing very well with his life, and is very much aware of what beliefs he has in himself, about himself, and about other people.

A young woman I had known for several years was puzzled because every time she started to develop a serious relationship with a young man, it never seemed to have any permanence. She wondered if there was something wrong with her that turned men off, or chased them away. I had known her for a long time so I said, "Listen Debbie, every time you talked to me about a new boy friend he was the most fantastic, stupendous, wonderful young man you ever had met in your life, and I would say to myself, 'Oh gosh, here we go again.' Now, I must admit over the past years your ability to select finer men to be involved with has greatly improved. Now, what do you really want out of a relationship with a man?"

"I want him to be committed to me until it ends."

"Did you hear what you just said? You have a fixed idea that every relationship will end. Therefore without realizing it, you are perpetuating your own self-fulfilling prophecy. You won't give of yourself to make the relation-

ship last or work because you think it's going to end
anyway."

The power of fixed beliefs and ideas are not just one
idea that a person can have in his mind, but they can be
reinforced and built upon, until he has literally built a
wall around himself.

A young woman was in therapy because she realized
that her demanding, jealous, non-trusting behavior had
caused her nothing but grief and she wanted to change.
She had a lifelong pattern of not trusting people, of being
overly possessive in a relationship, and of being extremely
jealous and demanding. I knew that she had been programmed very powerfully to have these beliefs implanted
in her mind.

The homework I assigned her was to allow her mind
to wonder about what messages she had received from
her mother and father, or other significant adults, about
not trusting people. At first she was blank. I told her not
to think about it but to just go home and wonder. Then
she said, "I really can't recall many things from my
childhood memories. I came along late in my parents' life.
I try to remember, but I can't." I asked her just to give
her memory permission to recall the messages.

Later that week I received a phone call from her and
she reported excitedly, "Listen to what I remembered from
my mother's warnings to me—'Don't trust anyone, not
even your father,' and 'Remember, the devil never sleeps.'
My father's message was, 'Don't trust anyone, not even
a priest.' " These were powerful statements that became
fixed ideas.

Her mother and father never trusted each other either,
because he was continually having affairs with other

women. If she couldn't see trust between her parents, and they told her not to trust, growing up in that kind of home must have been very powerful and destructive. She believed her parents, and the belief that she should never trust anyone became a fixed idea implanted in her mind.

The pain of losing another relationship that was very important to her helped her work very hard to challenge those basic fixed beliefs and to relax and believe in herself.

Have you ever taken time to be truly alone with yourself and let your mind wonder and wander? Try to think of the things you would like to change within yourself, and then listen very carefully to the inner dialogue which will counterattack your desire to change things about yourself. Sometimes it is very hard to listen to ourselves.

I look at the human mind as if it is a huge computer and memory bank. We have stored within our memory bank of the mind, all of our memories, thoughts and ideas. A negative message is a series of negative thoughts that are based upon a very profound, powerful fixed idea. Once you begin to think about it, or push the "on" button, so to speak, these tapes take over. They can start not only with the thoughts, but they produce bad emotions, and then recall bad memories.

Take time to search for those thoughts and fixed ideas. I admit that some people say, "But they are so much a part of me. I can't change." As long as you believe that, you won't change, but negative tapes and beliefs only have power over your life by your permission and acceptance of them. That's placing quite a bit of responsibility on you, but it also is offering you a great deal of hope.

Freddie was a young twelve-year-old boy who had a learning disability. He was well-built, athletic and very nice looking. He looked normal, like every other kid in his classroom, except there was something wrong in his neurological development. He had a hard time reading and his concentration wasn't the greatest.

His teacher would say, "All right, I want this assignment started now, and you're to finish it in twenty minutes." He would start but he never could finish in the allotted time. The teacher would get very upset with him, and he would get angry with the teacher and act up in class. Before he knew it, he had been sent down to the principal's office.

He had started getting some additional help—a special education class for his reading disability. However, the thing that concerned me was that he was beginning to believe that he was no good. He was living with a very powerful "I hate my teacher" tape.

I asked Freddie to come in and talk about it honestly. I explained to him what a negative tape was and how it was a bummer; that he didn't have to allow that tape to destroy his life. I said, "Would you like to have a good time in school—maybe even freak out your teacher's mind—making her wonder what's happened to you? I believe that if we can teach you the art of breaking up the negative tapes and how to control your own thoughts, you'll be able to do quite well. First of all, I want you to smile at her a lot!"

"Smile at her! Yuk! I hate her!"

"No, be still a minute. I want you to smile at her, and she won't know why. She'll wonder what you've been up to. What you're going to smile about is that you're imagining she's a witch and you've hidden her broom. She'll have no way to get home, but she doesn't know it yet." He laughed and said he thought it was a funny idea!

Monday he went back to school and tried the smile bit. When he came in to see me the next week, I asked him how things were going.

"I smiled, smiled and kept smiling all week, until the teacher didn't know what to do with smilin' Freddie. She kept wondering when I was going to act up and be wild and nasty! The other day she gave her usual assignment and limited the time. I thought I'd make a fool of myself again, but I was hanging loose. Do you know what, Doc? I finished it just like every other kid." He was grinning from ear to ear. "I realize now that all that time I spent hating her, I was draining away my energy to get the work done. I need to pay attention as hard as I can to make it through this class. I'm going to keep right on smiling, but I'll never tell her why I'm smiling."

Why are some people afraid to love? I'm sure you have heard the standard clichés like, "You may get hurt," or, "Love demands too much of a responsibility to engage in a loving relationship." But often there are very deep reasons why a person is afraid to love.

A woman was in therapy because she was having a difficult time responding sexually to her husband. We talked about how she had been programmed to think about sex, and what her mother had told her. Among other things, she revealed that by the time she was dating she was made to feel that sex was dirty and something that "nice people" never enjoyed. In subtle ways she had been programmed to believe that it was awful!

When I asked her about her relationship with her father, she described him as a very unpredictable, and yet rather charming individual. No one ever knew when he was going to show up. Sometimes he would be gone for two or three weeks at a time and then just appear at the door. She loved him very much, but was never sure of his love. When he died suddenly, she had still never really resolved in her own mind where she stood with her father.

Then we talked about her own marriage. I asked why she was afraid to open up and give her love fully to her husband now. She let this fixed idea slip, "Oh, it doesn't make much difference. He's only going to leave me anyway."

"Did you hear what you just said! 'He's going to leave me anyway.' If you're afraid to be open with him and enjoy a loving relationship, the fixed idea that he's going to leave you anyway is your protective device, to keep you shielded from the time you feel he will leave you. But in the meantime, what has it brought you? It's brought you nothing but frustration, loneliness and tenseness in the relationship. You're basing it on the very profound belief that he will leave you, just like your father did."

This is the story of a man's inner belief of who he was. Several years ago I was asked to do an intelligence test and neurological evaluation of a young man. Before we began the series of testing, he said, "Doc, do you think the fact that I just returned from my father's funeral on the coast would have any effect on the test results?"

I said "It sure would. How did your father die?"

"He blew his brains out with a shotgun."

His father had been an alcoholic for many years and it was alcoholism that caused the breakup of his parents' marriage. After the divorce his father stopped drinking, became very much involved in AA, remarried and had become a very successful business man in California. The mother also remarried and strangely enough the two families were friendly with each other. There was no animosity.

With thirteen years of sobriety under his belt, the father returned one day to Phoenix to pick up his son and said, "Drive me to my home down in New Mexico." The son drove part of the way and then his father insisted on driving. He drove like a madman, going at speeds of over 100 miles an hour and taking chances. His son thought at any moment there would be a horrible accident.

When he entered his home, he sat down and asked for a drink. After all these years of sobriety, his son could not believe his father would destroy himself after coming so far. He couldn't make him stop drinking or come back with him to Arizona. The son left his father at his parents' home in New Mexico and came back to Phoenix alone.

A week later his father stumbled into the son's house, dead drunk, and mumbled that he had been in Mexico. He couldn't remember how in the world he had gotten from Mexico to Phoenix.

It was a nightmarish trip back to California. His wife was shocked to see him devastated by his alcoholic condition. She had no indication of a problem and believed that they had a good marriage. He was very successful in his career, had received many promotions and even new responsibility. His wife was a nurse and tried to get him to go into a hospital, but he staunchly refused. His wife and son realized how self-destructive he was now, so they tried to empty the house of any possible weapons—guns and long knives.

In his melancholia, the father would sit in a chair and play the same record over and over again on the phonograph, saying to his son, "Hey, listen to this . . . this is really me . . . this is really who I am!" The record was *Skid Row Joe.* After a short while he found a disassembled shotgun that had been missed in the search and he blew his brains out.

How many times have you known a person who, from all outward appearances, was extremely successful, and when everything seemed to be going his way suddenly killed himself. Here was a successful man, a man who had been dry as an alcoholic for thirteen years and happily married. Why did he now destroy himself? He, himself, told us the secret—that in spite of success, sobriety and a good marriage, he had not changed his fixed ideas and belief about himself. His self-belief was that he was a no-good bum, a Skid Row Joe.

I want you to imagine your negative self-concept in one hand and your actual life in the other hand with imaginary rubber bands joining them. The higher your life ascends, the more successful you are, the greater the tension between the two. Finally, to reduce the tension, a person either has to change his fixed idea about his self-concept and make peace with himself, or he will do something drastic to reduce his high level of performance so that the tension will be less and he will be able to function.

In this case, the man's performance and his life became so high, that to relieve his tension he used a shotgun because he believed he was truly Skid Row Joe. As Linus once said, "Man's heaviest burden is his potential."

As a consulting psychologist I am able to meet a great number of professional people, particularly dentists. A curious aspect of the dental profession is that it has the highest suicide rate of the professions. Psychiatrists used to be in first place. I like to ease the sting somewhat by saying, "At least you're first in something!"

The dental profession is a high-stress one, filled with the pressure of producing work and maintaining standards of excellence. Yet they have people tell them day after day, "I hate dentists, but not you, personally." Still, it is very personal because it's their gut that hurts.

This is a deeper problem than most people realize because most dentists don't come from professional families. As studies have revealed, their professional life moves them up the success ladder far higher than their fathers ever achieved. Sometimes five years after dental school they are making more money than they ever dreamed of and more than their fathers.

A number of dentists have a "poor boy" concept. Unless they change that self-concept and give themselves permission to deserve the money they make, they will experience more and more tension and will look around for some way to reduce the tension through a bad investment, the breakup of a marriage through divorce or too much alcohol.

One day I received a phone call from a dentist I had known through the years and respected very much. He was very bright, sensitive and concerned about his professional growth. He had taken almost every course in continuing education that could be offered. He had it together as much as any successful dentist I had ever known, and was not a high fee dentist.

You can imagine my surprise when he called and said "Can I fly in from California and spend an afternoon with you in therapy?" I blocked out a Friday afternoon, but I must confess I couldn't imagine why Tom wanted to see me for counseling.

At lunch Tom said, "I don't know what it is that is really bothering me. My practice is going very well. My skills are excellent. My income has greatly increased and I'm doing the kind of dentistry that I really enjoy. I have a wonderful wife and family, a new Lincoln Continental, a lovely home and new swimming pool. I'm proud, really proud of the quality of work I do. But something is wrong deep inside and I can't figure it out. Why *now* of all times should I be filled with self-doubts and depression?"

I admitted that I was puzzled as to why he came to me, but I asked him off the wall so to speak, "Tom, where did you grow up? Tell me about your childhood. What did your dad do for a living?"

His face dropped immediately, and in a quiet voice he replied, "My father managed the county dump in a little town in Oregon, and we lived in there. Trash and broken toys were my playground. There is a smell about a dump that I thought would never wash from my skin."

At that point I think I understood Tom. I said "Once in a while as you lie by your beautiful pool in the back yard, you pick up a strange odor from that old county dump in Oregon and you feel uneasy. Maybe you feel guilty and wonder, 'What business does a poor boy like me have enjoying all this money, home, success, summer trips to Hawaii and the Caribbean? My father never really made it in life.' You begin to feel guilty because you prosper and your finances continue to grow and increase."

Tom quietly replied, "This must be the problem. I realize I feel guilty at times about all the success that has come my way."

"Tom," I replied, "no one gave you your success. You worked hard for it. You studied and were determined to provide the finest quality care for people who came to you for treatment as a dentist. If you and I wanted to be honest, and carry this even one step further, neither you nor I deserve all these good things in life because they come as so many gifts of God. So instead of feeling guilty, why not give thanks?"

So many of us have been work-oriented and programmed to always struggle hard and set more goals, that once we have reached our goals we have never been given permission to enjoy them and be thankful. Let's examine Linus' statement again. "Man's heaviest burden is his potential."

When I was a teenager, I stacked cement blocks every summer in Phoenix. One of the most important advantages of working in that desert heat, stacking blocks, is that by the end of the summer my callused, sore hands and aching muscles told me that I needed nothing else to motivate me to continue my education. Every summer the fellows I worked with would say "Kenny, are you going back to school again this fall?" I would reply, "You had better believe it!"

I knew that I would not want to be a laborer the rest of my life. My job also made me appreciate a college education because it was money that I had worked and sweated so hard for to go to college, and no way was I going to blow it!

One thing which perplexed me was how someone could stay at the same repetitive job day after day and year after year? I used to stop and visit with my old fellow workers in the summertime, just to stay in touch with them and talk about old times. I think the reason for their ability to stay at the block plant was that their potential and level of performance in life were about equal. I found that a person can have a much more difficult time with his life if he has a high potential and he knows it, but his performance level in life is not even close to his potential.

This type of person can find school so easy that he can do very little work rather quickly. With little effort he can learn just enough to get by and get good grades without ever challenging himself to think or discipline his mind. Often this person will become easily bored with school and will be brighter than his teacher. To break up boredom he sometimes will act up and get into trouble. He may get straight A's in all of his subjects, but F's in citizenship.

It's easy to blame the school systems for not motivating that kind of person. But each person motivates himself. School gives you the opportunity to read, to grow and to think. Schoolwork for a high-potential person is not that demanding, so it's possible to do the required work quickly and then study what you really want to learn. Going to school gives us a chance to grow intellectually that we may not have later when we are earning a living and supporting a family.

One of the biggest problems a high-potential person has to deal with is a heavy psychological problem diagnosed as laziness and mental sloppiness. If things come to easily, it can stop a person from stretching himself, from setting high enough goals; from disciplining his mind to work to grow and develop the potential that is in himself.

How frustrating it is for a person to know that he can do many things very well, yet has never learned to discipline his mind and his actions because he has always taken the easy and quick way out so he can just get by. The word discipline is kind of dirty in today's language with the now-culture and instant sensations. Why worry? Why sweat? Why think about the future? Discipline simply means to learn, to be able to set goals, to be able to structure time.

One of my secrets was learning to develop a self-discipline. My junior year in college I took twenty-one hours. I was in a hurry to get through school, I admit. I made these two things my rules for the semester: (1) I would have a good grade average, since it was my money that was paying tuition, and I felt good when I got good grades; (2) From 5 P.M. Friday afternoon until Monday afternoon, I would never open a book, because I wanted to be free to have fun, because I was already engaged to the woman who later became my wife. I decided which hours were to be blocked out for school work and which ones were to be used for leisure. I really lived with those decisions, because once you make them you don't have to keep making them over and over again.

Another thing I learned was that procrastination was a drag on my mind; it meant that I always had unfinished or deferred projects hanging in the back of my mind, haunting me. I didn't want that so I finally developed a regular schedule of study, workouts in the gym and weekends of leisure; and I really held to it.

I also followed the psychological principle that when I was doing intensive study and learning, I should allow that learning to become a part of me by doing something that was just the opposite. I found dating a very beautiful woman an extremely diverting pastime!

I followed this schedule even during finals week. I never studied on the weekends. Apparently, my method was successful since I got all A's and two B+'s. I can even play the Ain't Fair Blues because I didn't think it was fair I got the two B+'s. Somebody might say I was lucky or that I was brilliant, but it wasn't either luck or brilliance. It was merely that I could say no to some things and yes to others.

If you don't learn this, especially if you have high potential, your potential and your performance probably won't match. Because you'll be in conflict with yourself and because you can't lie to yourself, you'll feel tension within you. When you are performing somewhere within the range of your potential, you'll feel that good feeling of self-fulfillment that only you can give yourself.

If we could discipline our lives and use our minds more creatively, life would not be so boring. One time I was in Yuma, Arizona, talking to a group of high school seniors on drug-abuse education day, when one of the students stood up and said, "But Dr. Olson, Yuma is a very boring town!" I said, "In your sixteen years, if you haven't found within you the resources and the abilities to find something exciting and creative and fun in life, then I'm sorry. It isn't Yuma that's boring. It's *you* that is boring!"

The Rent-a-Cross Program

I admit that there are some people who, no matter how much you praise them, or tell them their work is beautiful, or *they* are beautiful, say, "No it isn't. It's really nothing. Just the Nobel Prize, really nothing at all!" No matter what they do or how they are praised, they cut themselves down.

One time I had a conversation with a man who I sensed was a very destructive name-caller, and I asked him about it. He said he was and then I asked what he called himself.

"Dumb shit," he said.

"You do?"

"Yeah. In fact, I'm president of the Dumb Shit Club of America."

I was really shocked when he reached into his billfold and pulled out a business card which had his name and the statement "President, Dumb Shit Club of America." I laughed hard at this because this man had found a secret. Instead of doing the name-calling, self-persecuting thing, he accepted it and turned it into a joke, and then he could hang loose.

I will never forget "The Peanut Butter Princess" who was young, attractive and thoroughly delightful. When she found out I was a shrink, she told me some of her life story. She had an unbelievable sense of humor. I couldn't imagine how she could have a problem, but she said even though she'd been in analysis for years, nothing seemed to help her. She described some of the fun she had with people, and that she was thinking of writing a book titled, Cooking with Peanut Butter and signing it

"The Peanut Butter Princess." I told her she had the secret right there—it was her laughter. This should keep her from being uptight and down on herself.

"Even when I used to see my analyst," she said, "I would go in and sit there very woodenly, stiff and with my hair pulled back very tightly. He would get so nervous he would say, 'My goodness, please relax. You make me so nervous!' Then I would tell him that I was relaxed, but that he should see me when I'm really uptight!" You have to admit that when someone can even put her analyst "on" she has real class!

Then she went on to tell me, "I have this inner dialogue going on inside me. I can laugh and I can have fun. I can do all these great things. I enjoy life and I enjoy people, but there is another side of me too. When it starts its dialogue . . ."

Then I interrupted her momentarily to say, "It's a tape, you mean."

She agreed and went on to say that when she turned on the tape, she would persecute herself for all the things she had done wrong for the past ten years.

"What kind of instructions did you get from your parents about the kind of life you should lead?"

"Well, my parents always told me not to try anything unless I was the best."

Now I've got news for you. That's a real setup for failure and misery. You can't always be the best at everything, and with that criteria there is no credit for being second or taking an honorable mention. Naturally, she rebelled against it.

She told me she had done some dumb things, some bad

and destructive things. Consequently she brooded over the past ten years.

"Now, wait a minute!" On one hand you have this tremendous ability to make other people laugh, and even to laugh at yourself. Yet, on the other, you seem to hang onto the persecution, the self-flagellation. I have a solution for you because I really think that you'd rather do the masochism bit than to enjoy life. I suggest that you invest in the 'Rent-a-Cross Program.' "

"What do you mean by that?"

"I want you to set up a big cross that you can climb up on when you get home at night so that you can suffer for all your sins. Have somebody nail you up there, and you can hang all night. Really persecute yourself so that when you go to work you can be free after you've done penance."

She could do nothing but laugh!

I did this for a real purpose because one of the best ways to break up a very destructive tape is to place in the midst of that tape a powerful imagery that will just literally blow the fuse on that tape and wipe it out. Whenever she thought about how terrible she was, she would always think that maybe she ought to go rent a cross, and would laugh at our conversation.

I was back in that town six weeks later and I met her again. She was radiant and full of life. I had told the story of our first meeting on television, and had let her know when it would be aired so that she could watch the show. She was thrilled to tell me how much she had changed, which she did with her usual good humor.

"I told my friends I was going to give up smoking cigarettes for Lent. They all agreed it would be difficult, but I said it wouldn't be hard for me because I didn't smoke. Then I decided I would make a real sacrifice and give up eating peanut butter, which I eat at least three times a day. Even that wasn't enough, so I finally settled on giving up self-pity."

The power of her change was so evident that people couldn't believe she could change so much in such a short time. But when she broke up her negative tapes she destroyed her old fixed ideas that were destroying her. She told me she was thinking of writing her analyst for a refund of the thousands of dollars she spent for nothing!

The Torture of Self-Doubting Masculinity or Femininity

Homosexuality has been pretty much a taboo topic for discussion until recent times. From a professional point of view, in training and in the reading I've done through the years, my impression had been that homosexuality was a hopeless area of behavioral change. Now I have good reason to believe that the main problems we have with homosexuality are our beliefs that it is hopeless, and in our failure to discriminate between various types of homosexual behavior.

Let me make it very clear that I'm not generalizing, but that I'm just trying to illustrate again how the power of a fixed idea—an event, and then a self-recrimination—can be very destructive for a person.

Usually what I find is this kind of pattern. Sometimes a young boy in growing up is afraid of his father because his father is a bully and controls him through fear. Naturally, the boy rebels against him. When he reacts against his father in such a way, his subconscious mind may play a trick on him and tell him that to be a man is to be like his father. He doesn't want to be like his father at all.

Very often when I ask when the first homosexual experience occurred, he will describe it as a time right before or at the beginning of puberty, usually a seduction by an older man. From that one event he feels sexual excitement, but following that there is guilt and tremendous self-condemnation.

Adolescence for a boy is a really shaky time as far as sexual identity is concerned. One of the major goals of adolescence is being able to make it from the world of being with just boys to enjoying, developing and understanding what it is like to have healthy heterosexual relationships with girls.

Some boys lack confidence and play the self-doubt tape, along with the "what if" tape—"What if I'm not a man? What if I'm not strong enough? What if girls don't like me?"

Then they begin to draw conclusions, their brooding feeds their fears and their self-doubts and inadequacies and builds a fixed idea that they're different—they're queer—they're homosexual. They may even attempt dating, but because of the negative tapes, just freeze in the experience. This again gives them a negative feeling.

However, I have found that if they say they want to change and reflect on why they have been thinking that way, they can start to turn off some of the negative tapes.

The next step is to help a person listen to himself and find the trigger words that start a pattern that leads him to a homosexual encounter. Then he can learn to say no to his impulse and wait.

An example of this phenomenon was a young man

who had been arrested. He decided he wanted to change and was able to break up his pattern of thinking rather successfully. One day he came in for therapy and said, "Doc, I'm really excited! Today at college I found myself looking at girls, not guys!" He began to believe in himself, and to develop more skills of communication so he could talk to girls. As he grew and expressed more self-confidence, he finally found a girl friend. Later he finished college and got married. This has also happened with other people when they realize that they have chosen homosexuality as a means of self-destruction.

Cursed by Fixed Ideas of Death, Fear and Guilt

In the late spring of the year a thirty-nine-year-old businessman, in a soft but tense voice, told me "I'm going to die on July 7, when I'm forty years old."

"I'm curious how you selected forty as the time you will die," I replied.

"Well, my older brother died of a heart attack when he was forty, and I guess all of my life I have been afraid of death. It's been a real big hangup with me. The older you get the more it becomes a reality."

"Well," I said, "we'll have to work very hard to find out how you were programmed about death, so we can break the spell before July 7 since I'm leaving on vacation the fourth of July.

Jerry, as I soon discovered, was not only cursed with fixed ideas about death but also about fear and guilt. What an unholy threesome they made—these three fixed ideas with a core of very destructive, negative tapes.

Jerry was born on a farm in South Dakota, somewhat of a surprise baby to his parents. His mother was about forty-two at the time and was the one who programmed his fears. She was afraid of everything and passed these fears on to Jerry. A young child can't defend himself against his parents' programming about death, fear and guilt.

Jerry was very close emotionally to his mother and never strayed too far away from her because he felt safe by her side. And yet, ironically, a child can also feel an eerie responsibility that as if by some magical power within him, he is supposed to be mother's guardian and protector as well.

One of Jerry's earliest memories was of his mother getting ready for Christmas and remarking as she got out the decorations, "Well, I made it to another Christmas. I wonder if I will still be here next year?"

He also vividly remembers a three-way discussion with his cousin, who was about the same age as Jerry, while his mother was doing the ironing, on "why we have to die." Mom said, "It's God's will that we die because we are all sinners." There was a very strong religious background for Jerry to live with, which tormented him.

The curse of this type of programming is that a child always lives with the expectation that something awful is about to befall him, especially if he doesn't obey his mother. The communications that program a person's life are usually done in an indirect way and on the edge of awareness. Too often the major traumatic events in life are blamed for emotional difficulties.

I have discovered that many people can deal more effectively with major crises than with the constant subtle ways they are told they're inferior, they're no good by inference or by double-bind messages. Jerry was not given direct instructions by his mother to be preoccupied with death, to do bad things so he would feel guilty, and to be afraid of leaving home and flying in an airplane.

The disturbing event that crystalized his fear of death into a fixed idea happened when Jerry was about ten years old. All he remembers is that he was pulling a wagon close to his home and he passed out. He didn't know how long he was unconscious, but only that he awakened in his bed. He looked at his hands and they seemed to appear yellow—like a dead man's hands, he thought. In panic he ran into the kitchen and said, "Mom, I'm going to die! Look at my hands! Mom, I'm going to die!" His mother agreed, "Yes, you are probably going to die."

From that day forward, Jerry lived under the ominous cloud of death. The nights became ordeals of terror and panic. He would search carefully under his bed each night to make sure that all was safe. His fear became so great that he slept with his mother until he was about fourteen. It was too frightening for him even to conceive the idea of spending the night at his brother's home, even though he liked him very much.

In retrospect, Jerry remarked that when other people read about an automobile accident or plane crash or other tragedy, they believed those kinds of events happened to other people, not themselves. He felt just the opposite and imagined the worst things happening to him. When he was young he could hardly stand it when someone other than a family member drove the car, and imagined every other car on the road about to run into them. He literally expected to die any minute. Try living with those negative tapes!

His older brother did a lot of flying and this worried

his mother very much. She passed her fear of flying on to him. She was so morbid about death that he remembered her making statements like, "I sure hope he makes it this time." Or, "He'll probably die in a crash. I'm glad I don't have to fly!" With programming like that, even though he intellectually knew that flying was much safer than driving, Jerry drove to his appointments everywhere rather than fly. He drove all the way home as if he would be able to ward off some calamity that might strike his home while he wasn't there.

Jerry's fear of flying was tied into his fixed idea about death. Can you imagine what it's like to lie awake all night, believing that this is your last night alive?

When Jerry was twenty-three-years-old he found that he was suffering from hypertension and, after extensive testing was told it had no organic basis. His physician said his emotional life was in such turmoil he should go for psychotherapy. He saw a psychologist for a number of years, and in time his blood pressure was normal again. He was not concerned about his heart until his brother died at forty from a coronary. Now that he was turning forty, his fixed idea told him that he was going to die of a heart attack, just like his brother.

Intertwined with his fixed ideas of death and fear was the fixed idea of guilt. Unfortunately for Jerry, his exposure to Christianity when he was growing up was as a religion of fear, of sin and guilt. God, in Jerry's eyes, must have been seen as a cosmic killjoy, who was always snooping around to see if anyone was having fun, so he could put a stop to it. Playing cards, going to the movies, going with a girl, in fact anything that may have been enjoyable, was sinful!

One of Jerry's biggest hangups about Christianity is guilt about being a rich man. The quotation, that it's harder for a rich man to get into heaven than for a camel to go through the eye of a needle, affected Jerry as a young businessman. He worked hard—after all that's part of his programming too—but as he earned another promotion and made a little more money, instead of feeling good, he would have a guilty feeling. Then came the day that he was making more money than he'd ever imagined he could. He wasn't a rich man yet, but the thought had hit him that he was close to being a rich man, and rich men don't go to heaven!

When you have to work your own way to heaven, it's really an impossible dream. Jerry remembered when he was a young boy, his older brother was going out at night with girls, drinking beer and having a good time. He prayed that when he grew up that he would not do such sinful things. He would be perfect! But as he looks back on things, his brother turned out to be a nice guy. He realized also *he* could never be perfect either.

Jerry said that he could spot which negative tape was playing by the part of his body that was having physical symptoms. When his arms became very tired, and the muscles in his neck and shoulders became tense, then he would ask himself what he was feeling guilty about. If he missed church for a couple of weeks, then he realized he must be being punished by guilt for not going to church every Sunday, because he was a sinner. If his heart began to pound, it was the death fixed idea. If he got the panicky feeling of not being home for a night, it was a fixed idea of fear.

Jerry realized that the fear of not getting home every

night was tied in to his fear of being too successful in business. If he could stay over another night in town, he could do a better job with his client, and thus be more successful.

Jerry made a great deal of progress in diffusing the power of his fixed ideas of death, fear and guilt. Coming back to that first incident when he passed out while pulling the wagon, I asked him casually if he had ever had any problems with reading in school.

He looked quite shocked, and said, "I always had a problem with reading. I never was a good reader. In fact, I used to have dreams at night that I was in church with about 300 people. I always had the dreaded fear that the pastor would single me out of all those people, to come and read something out of the Bible in front of everybody. It just terrified me because I just hate to read."

"Jerry, nobody's ever really explained to you that, as a growing young boy, you might have had a neurological developmental problem. Sometimes when boys are growing up their bodies are growing faster than their nerves can grow and the nerves occasionally will short circuit and they will pass out and faint. A minimal neurological problem can also be the cause for you having a difficult time learning to read. When you woke up and looked at your hands, it was so mysterious and awesome, and no one ever explained it to you. You probably felt it must be like dying."

"Yes, I woke up every morning for years and looked to see what color my hands were." Then he said, "Do you really mean that a neurological problem could cause just a small short circuit in the brain and it might just happen once?"

"Yes, and once it happened you felt you were dying. It was confirmed by your mother and became a fixed idea. You see, once we jump to conclusions about something and we don't know all the evidence, we end up with a very destructive, powerful fixed idea."

Jerry did not die on July 7, and he was free to live beyond that date. The following February though, he called for an appointment, and he was depressed again. I asked him about the significance of February. He said "My brother died in February. I'm withdrawing from people—in fact I can't even go out to lunch with a client."

"All right. Did your brother have his heart attack at lunch?"

"Yes, he did. As I was eating I had the weird thought that I had no right to enjoy lunch. There goes that tape again!"

I thought for a minute and then told Jerry he had certainly come a long way in breaking the curse of his fixed ideas. However, I thought we needed to name that fear tape. So after some consultation, we came up with the name "Little Freaky Freddie."

The next week he came back and said, "Doc, it's really working! I tell Little Freaky Freddie not to bother me, that I don't have time to waste on him. I'm much too busy getting back to normal."

Jerry was also instructed to open up with his wife when these weird, fixed ideas were bugging him, and not to leave her in the dark. He said, "I used to feel ashamed to talk about these strange thoughts. Now that I've got them into the open, it sure is better. My wife is relieved, and it helps to share a burden with somebody."

Jerry was also able to get his theology straightened out and to see God as a God of love and not of fear and death. That God loves us because we can't earn His respect or salvation by working our way into heaven. "What a relief," Jerry said, "to count on God's love instead of earning your own way."

Jerry has also learned to know what times of the year to be on guard. The summer is a good time for him, but he admits that he has to be very careful around the first of the year because these old tapes will come back to haunt him. He also realizes that life has cycles. A person can have two good days, then a not so good day. He's now trying to start out each day by telling himself it's going to be a good day. And if he has a bad day, he's sure not going to let it ruin tomorrow.

To have positive fixed ideas can be a source of inner power for a person. We are what we believe. In thinking about my own programming, I remember as a little child my mother used to read the same story to me over and over again. It was *The Little Engine That Could.* You remember it. It was the story about the little engine that sees a train stopped and says, "Do you need help?" And the train says, "Yes, I'm broken down." The little engine says, "I'll pull you over the hill," and the big train says, "Well, you're pretty small." The little engine says, "Well, I think I can. I think I can." Finally it pulls the long train up the hill saying, "I think I can. I think I can." At last it goes over the hill and, as it goes down the other side to the village, it says joyously, "I thought I could. I thought I could, I thought I could."

I wonder how much ability to keep thinking "I can" and not letting anything stop me has been part of my programming. I think quite a bit!

From my father, I learned how to bounce. His construction company went bankrupt when I was thirteen. I was quite concerned about him and asked how he felt about being bankrupt. He said, "Well, I bounce well." Well, I've been fired a few times in my life, and I'm thankful I have learned how to bounce.

Destructive fixed ideas are very powerful in controlling a person's life, but they can be defused and the negative tape can be turned off. It's hard to measure how much mental and emotional energy is wasted each day by the power of negative fixed ideas.

I just wish I could communicate more effectively with you so you could experience the new surge of mental energy, emotional well-being, and new motivation for life that is available within yourself once you have broken out of the prison of destructive, fixed ideas. Once you can tune into the inner dialogue as you talk to yourself, dream dreams of the future, and not brood over miserable yesterdays, you can decide whether this inner dialogue is negative or positive. Remember, the inner dialogue belongs to you. You turn it on and you can push the "off" button. No one can do it for you.

I have seen people change dramatically for the good in a short time. Marcus Aurelius said a long time ago, "The world in which we live is determined by our thoughts." A person can change the way he thinks about himself and his world. Time and again I ask a person to stop and wait one second and *think*. "Is this what I want to say? Do I want to allow this event or person to make me feel this way? Am I about to react or act in the way that's best for me?" Asking yourself these kind of questions is one way to break out of negative and habitual ways of reacting which do not take conscious effort.

If you have a poor self-concept then decide to get rid of it. Take the "t" out of can't and believe you can. No one can give you a new self-concept or a new positive idea about yourself, so if you are waiting for someone to give you a "new you" for Christmas or your birthday, forget it!

How can you get a good self-concept? First, decide that you want one.

Second, begin today to dream and fantasize about the "new you." Picture yourself doing the things that would enhance your self-respect. Begin to develop a powerful fixed idea of yourself in a positive way. Every time you hear a negative tape start, tell yourself to stop the old tune. It's done enough damage already.

Third, begin to set reachable goals that will make you feel good about yourself. You don't have to shout it from the housetops when you do a positive thing for yourself but be sure to give yourself credit for trying for doing things that will make you feel good. This is the secret of love. Love gives a powerful feedback to the self. In fact, love in this light is a selfish act. When you reach out and love someone, that person will benefit from being loved, but you are richer because in order to keep love, you have to give it away.

It is important to remember that what you consider reachable goals may appear as unimportant goals to someone else, but that's not your problem. Let me give you an illustration.

Since I was once a shy person I have a natural empathy for shy people. With a shy teenager we assign a series of small tasks that are easy to accomplish and yet help reach the goal of building new self-confidence. I ask that each time he starts a conversation with someone at school he is to mark it down on a piece of paper so he san keep a tally of how often he is asserting himself. The content of the conversation isn't important but the asserting of oneself is the goal. The marks provide immediate feedback which says, "I'm changing. I'm doing better. I did it."

I also try to find a person's strong points so he can build from strength and abilities he already possesses. Sometimes an individual is blind to his talents and good points, or he doesn't think they count.

The crime against self is committed when we won't give ourselves credit for the good things we do but remember only the mistakes. Write a list of the talents and good things you would like to try and accomplish. Remember, there is more gold in you than you believe. It's there! Go find it!

Teenagers aren't the only people whose low self-concept makes them feel inadequate and shy with people. A twenty-eight-year-old bachelor came for help. He was particularly shy with women and afraid his inexperience would soon be discovered on a date. We would role play on how to start a conversation and keep it going.

The first relief he experienced was when I told him the burden of the communication didn't rest only on his shoulders, but was equally shared. Soon he began to realize that he didn't need a "big line" to impress women, but they would see him as a great conversationalist because he learned how to ask open-ended questions that couldn't be answered with a yes or no. In essence, he became a good listener. We also had him practice talking with girls at work and having lunch with them. His strong point was tennis and this provided him a natural for finding a female partner.

When he went to a party he was instructed to look for the shyest girl there. He was to approach this person, introduce himself and tell her how shy he was and how hard it was for him to come over and introduce himself. A whole conversation can be built around overcoming shyness.

The secret of the successful person is his ability to recognize his own strengths and weaknesses, his powerful fixed ideas about himself and his ability to learn new behavior and be a problem solver. A very unusual ability of successful people is that they take time out to *think*. Failure is not seen as a disaster but only an indication to seek other solutions. A successful person is one with strong personal commitments and inner beliefs. J.S. Mills once remarked "One person with a belief is equal to a force of ninety-nine who have only interest."

Another characteristic of a successful person is his ability to wait for the right time. People with less belief and commitment will give up too soon because they are unable to handle the frustration of waiting and the ensuing tension that is created by not being able to finish a task or reach a goal as soon as expected.

The ability to wait, to be patient and then, when the time is right, to act is best described in the words of Benjamin Disraeli who said, "There is nothing more powerful than the idea whose time has come."

6

SAD SONGS AND SUICIDE

*There are so many sad songs written because
there are so many sad people in the world.*

I heard this as I was listening to the music on a headset
while flying across the country. It has been reported that
depression is so widespread the National Institute of
Mental Health estimates that twenty million Americans
suffer from a serious depression each year. As widespread
as depression is, it is still underdiagnosed, undertreated
and misunderstood. The term depression is too global.
What is needed is for us to recognize the symptoms and
the varieties of depression.

Definition of Despair

There is a difference between despair and depression.
Despair is the human cry of pain because a loved one
has died, a romance has ended, or a person is suddenly
afflicted with a disabling illness.

Despair is the result of the hard knocks of life and the emotional response to these blows. The pain is real but a person finds the strength in time to go on living and he doesn't allow the despair to turn into a life style of depression.

Despair is the realization and awareness that life comes with a full range of emotional experiences—from joy to pain, to laughter and tears, to triumphs and fears. The times of despair are hard, but they do help a person treasure the joys and highs of life and sometimes jolt a person into reexamining the priorities in his life.

Symptoms of Depression

The symptoms of depression include many signs. A person may develop a long-standing life-style of depression when he believes he is not lovable or when he has been hurt. The theme song for him could be *Alone Again, Naturally*. There is a deep feeling of personal inadequacy and fear that if someone ever became intimate with him the horrible truth would be discovered that he wasn't much at all.

Thus for protective purposes people build walls around themselves. These walls not only keep others out, but become a prison for the person who can't or won't leave the prison. True, such a person is safe, but alone and living out a life of no love.

Once in a while he may risk exposing himself to other people to see if there is anyone who could love him, but he sets himself up for rejection and does things to test the other person's love until the situation becomes impossible. So back he goes to the prison walls and a deep depression!

Love for a depressed person is being loved enough by others to feel worthwhile. Love is not seen by him as an active process of reaching out, giving and caring for others, but rather as standing on a street corner waiting for the streetcar named "Love" to stop.

Depression is a decision of hopelessness; of giving up responsibility for one's life. Once this happens, the prison doors are locked from the *inside*. Life is acted out in slow motion. Everything is too much effort. Life is boring and there is no motivation or ambition. Friends offer a thousand helpful solutions but not one works.

Either he wants to sleep all the time only to waken and not feel rested, or at night he wakes up at two or three A.M., his mind racing with thoughts and unable to get back to sleep.

To find the way out of depression a person often places his hope in pills and alcohol. These help him forget for a short time, but too often the "cure" becomes a curse. He refuses to take personal responsibility for changing his life and wants a pill, a person or a miracle to save him. As long as a depressed person has a fixed idea of hopelessness he will live out his self-fulfilling prophecy and may even resort to suicide as the way to end the depression.

Once a depressed person begins to hope, to believe in himself and take a personal responsibility for his life then there is the dawn of a new day.

Self-Pity Depression

Self-pity depression plays *The Ain't Fair Blues* as a negative tape. Once the "on" button is pushed, a person begins to brood about all the things that haven't been fair in his past. The longer the brooding, the more the person sinks into a quagmire of self-pity. While indulging in self-pity you can almost hear a phonograph in the background playing *Born To Lose*. Self-pity depression is a good people-repellant since no one wants to be around someone indulging in self-pity.

What someone talks about is a good clue to his emotional life. If he dwells only on *The Ain't Fair Blues* then that's how he will feel. If he shuts up and turns off the negative tapes he will feel better quickly. So will those around him!

Depression as Anger Turned Inward

Another form of depression is anger that has been turned inward. The person has been programmed not to express anger and has had no permission to ventilate his frustrations. There are no good or bad emotions because emotions are realities; they are facts. When anger is turned inward, deep depression is the result.

The inability to express anger may also result in physical symptoms such as bottled-up anger locked in the joints of the knees or in persistent headaches. This type of depression can be difficult to help in therapy because so often the source of anger and frustration is blocked out and the underlying depression is seldom dealt with therapeutically.

One of the most difficult persons I ever tried to work with was a teenager by the name of Janie. Her depression was so all-encompassing that it was evident in her body posture, her long silences and her inability to talk. Long hours were spent trying to have her verbalize, but she would control the relationship with silence. I'd feel so frustrated I'd tell her that if she didn't want to talk I might as well read a book or write a letter, which often I would do.

In an attempt to have Janie physically express her bottled-up anger I asked her to strike my hand, but as usual, she refused to cooperate. I took her hand and, instead of striking mine, she pulled back. I found that she was an expert in fighting backwards. Not only that, she was a very strong young woman. After forty-five minutes of struggling, her appointment was over, and Janie went home.

Her mother phoned me later and reported that whatever took place during her session worked, because she had not seen Janie so happy in a long time. I wish I could report that from that day on therapy made great strides, but it didn't. In time I discharged her and we both agreed that therapy had not been beneficial to her.

Four years later Janie called me for an appointment. She sounded very desperate so I agreed to see her again. She was not as withdrawn into her depression as before but was now very suicidal. She told of several suicide attempts and realized that she was even a failure in killing herself. I remarked that she shouldn't feel badly about that because some people just have no talent for suicide.

Janie had made some friends, was living on her own and working. I agreed to give her several weeks to think about whether or not she really wanted to change. During the following weeks she lost her job and had to face the reality of going back to a very dysfunctional home that was like slow quicksand for her.

In one of our talks she began to verbalize some of her raw anger and panicked at the rage she felt inside. Suddenly she cried out and ran for the door. I caught her and held her tightly so I could try to calm her down. At that moment she would have killed herself. As we stood in my office I heard her fingering the letter opener on my desk. It was then I realized that she was pondering whether or not to stab me in the back. In my training and reading I was not prepared to deal with the moment when someone was ready to stab me. All I could do was hold her and reassure her that she would not fall apart and that she would be all right. I was more than a little relieved when she let go of the letter opener and relaxed.

How do I know she was thinking of stabbing me? My fears were justified when her pastor called me that evening after he had talked with her and she told him of her thoughts about killing me.

Janie was physically very strong. When she came for her appointment I told her I had made a serious mistake in that I had viewed her depression as weakness. Now I saw it as the focus of all her strength. She would do anything to keep from getting better!

Then I recalled that day four years ago when I wanted her to strike my hand and how she fought backwards and won. She never did strike my hand. As she remembered that day her eyes sparkled.

"I am now going to give you a new name," I said. "Muley. Anyone who is as stubborn as a mule to keep from getting better has to be recognized for that stubborn strength. It demands a great amount of energy through all these years to stay depressed. You will do anything to keep from having fun, keeping a job, loving a friend or being proud of yourself."

I also told her that if she ever used her strength and

energy in a positive way in her life nothing could stop her because of her determination. Janie smiled and was pleased with her new name.

I asked her not to reject my idea before she heard me out. I suggested she investigate the armed forces and all the advantages the armed forces could offer her. Naturally, she had to first reject the idea. Before I knew it, she had not only investigated the advantages, but had joined the army.

I had not heard from Janie for about a year when I received a long distance call from her. Her voice rang with joy and life. She wanted to share the good news that she was to be married at Thanksgiving to a wonderful man she had met in the service. I wonder if he knew how stubborn she could be!

For people whose depression is anger turned inward I often suggest that they keep a note pad with them and write down at random what they are angry about and why they keep in all this anger. Punching bags and pounding on pillows also help. But they are warned that to finally let go of all that bottled-up pain and anger will be a painful experience, like lancing a boil. A boil has to be drained of its poison before healing can take place.

Depression from Guilt

Guilt can produce another form of depression. The syndrome of guilt can create a vicious cycle that has only a downward spiral. If someone makes you feel guilty, it hurts and the natural reaction is to strike out. Being hostile, however, can induce guilt which hurts and so goes the vicious cycle of guilt on its downward spiral.

The first type of guilt I would like to discuss is that of induced guilt. None of us enjoys feeling guilty, yet as parents we easily resort to guilt as a means to control our children. When the Los Angeles area was struck with earthquakes a few years ago there was the story of a mother who felt her home shake with a violent tremor. In her concern for the safety of her son she cried out, "Johnny!" His quick reply was, "I didn't do it, Mommy."

In order to program a child to live with guilt one must always use fear or respect for authority as motivators. Conditional love means that a child feels that no matter what he does it will not be good enough to win the approval and acceptance of his parents.

If guilt is used to control a young child, remember he will have a difficult time distinguishing between doing something bad and believing *he* is bad. For example, children, around the age of five are naturally curious about the differences in the anatomies of boys and girls. If their curious exploring should be suddenly interrupted by an irate parent who screams at the children that they are bad, the children wonder what the great crime was. They decide, "What we did was not that bad so *we* must be bad!"

Religions have long been making people feel guilty and afraid of God. Religion too often is reduced to a list of do's and don'ts which end up with far more don'ts than do's. Anytime a religion tells a person his salvation or acceptance by God is up to him and his ability to keep the rules of the religion, it's a sure-fire way to induce guilt and never feel at peace with oneself, much less with God.

From my point of view, authoritarian religious organizations are fear and guilt factories. It's no wonder that people get fed up with organized religions because they find so little love, acceptance, joy and abundant living. For me, being a Christian is to know and experience the love of God in Christ who loved and accepted me because I didn't deserve it, but I needed it. The curse of guilt is broken and a new life of love, joy and thanksgiving takes its place.

Guilt which produces depression also comes from incorrect decisions and beliefs about oneself. I once had as a patient a bright, attractive woman in her late 20s who suffered from periodic deep depression. She had been married several times and was currently earning a living as a prostitute. Her life style was very destructive. In a therapy group we began to talk about guilt, and Lupe began to tell of the burden she carried. We talked about what she could have done that would make her feel so guilty.

Finally she said that she had killed her two-year-old sister when she was five years old. It was as if an old door of her mind was opened after being locked shut for many years. I asked how she killed her sister. Lupe remembered that one time when she took her for a walk her sister fell. But did she die from the fall?

After a long silence she recalled a rainy night when her sister was very ill. A doctor was there and everyone was crying. I pushed her further to try and remember. Was it due to the fall? Finally she realized that the stormy night and the doctor had nothing to do with her sister falling down. I was puzzled now and tried to discover the reason for Lupe believing that she had killed her little sister.

The room was filled with an eerie quality as Lupe recalled the funeral; of how her sister was placed in a coffin that looked like a little carriage. People came to the house to cry and look at her sister.

I asked Lupe what she did during this time. She remembered going over to the coffin and touching her sister. Her sister's skin felt cold, so she looked up at her mother and saw a horrified look on her mother's face. She believed that her touch had killed her sister, and the look of shock on her mother's face confirmed her conclusion. With the guilt from this incorrect decision and belief, Lupe had spent her life punishing herself.

A person can feel guilt from violating one's moral and spiritual values. In this instance guilt can serve as a warning light to stop him from continuing to compromise himself and destroy his life. When a person has messed up his life he has the right to feel guilty. It can be therapeutic if it causes him to take stock and stop whatever he is doing that makes him feel guilty.

Here are a few suggestions on how to prevent a depression from guilt:

1. Decide to quit being a "blame blotter." This is one who has been programmed to accept the guilt for anything that goes wrong around him, whether it belongs to him or not.

2. Practice forgiveness. Try forgiving yourself. You just may like it. Don't try to upstage God by saying, "Well, He may forgive me but He doesn't know me like I do." Practice forgiveness with your children. When I would blow it as a parent I would go to the child I offended and ask for forgiveness. Children are so great. My kids would always forgive me and say, "That's all

right, Dad, we know you're messed up, but we love you."

3. If you have hurt someone, go to that person and ask for forgiveness. This is hard to do but it is a powerful way of getting rid of guilt.

4. If you need to talk with someone, find a person who has come to terms with his own humanness, his strengths and his weakness. Unload your guilt to that person. People who have needed forgiveness themselves are able to accept and understand another person's need for forgiveness.

Fatigue-Debt Depression

This is a form of depression that is most familiar to me. I have been known in the past to push myself too hard and too long until the only fuel I am running on is adrenalin. The main symptom is a feeling of being "wired" like a person on speed; I'm exhausted but have difficulty going to sleep. If I do get to sleep, I am awake at 2:30 or 3:00 A.M. and my mind is racing with thoughts. During this time I may also have a bad nightmare. I am easily irritated. My mind and body are telling me to be prepared for a fatigue-debt depression which forces me to slow down, do nothing, and sleep as much as I need to renew myself. I am like a rubber band that has been stretched and finally goes limp.

I have finally learned how to pace myself and listen to my body. I have also learned how to let go for fifteen minutes to an hour and go into a deep, trancelike state of complete relaxation. "Hanging loose" is certainly better than being strung out and "uptight."

Reactive Depression

Reactive depressions are the result of reactions to life's blows that don't stop with the anguish of despair, but go on to deeper levels and a life of being depressed.

Many forms of mild depression work their way out just with the passing of time. A father loses a job and withdraws into a shell of depression, but when he finds a new job his depression ends.

Young adults often experience a floundering depression when they finish high school, college or graduate school and then try to find a place of employment. It's a rather bitter pill to hear that you are over-qualified for a job and that there may not be a place for you.

It's hard to be over twenty-one and want to be out on your own, but still living at home. Parents need to be very understanding about the dilemma faced by young adults. They shouldn't worry about the young person never leaving home, but should instead be supportive and understanding. In time he will find a place for himself. This period of time will often be a time of depression that will be lifted by employment and seeing an opportunity for the future.

Reactive depressions can also be seasonal depressions. A special time of the year can bring on a reactive depression. One of the moods of Christmas is depression, especially if one is alone. Perhaps a loved one died during the year or around Christmas. It is a time of the year that triggers all kinds of memories.

As adults we often dread the coming of the holiday season and wonder why Christmas isn't like it was when we were children. When we were young the hardest thing we did was wait for the holidays. We didn't have to work to prepare for the big dinner or to worry about paying the bills for all the gifts. Psychologically, it is so easy to feel that our life will be different, that people will change and miracles will happen, but Christmas never quite meets our expectations. I dreamed of a *White Christmas* but all I got was the *Christmas Blues*.

This time of year people who are depressed should be very careful with alcohol. Too much alcohol only accentuates the underlying depression. Christmas can be a powerful time of renewal, of hope, of love, of gratitude and seeing a light shining in the darkness.

One of the most destructive reactive depressions is experienced in divorce. Men as well as women can be torn apart by the anguish, pain, rejection and anger precipitated by divorce. If a person has been married for twenty-five years, a divorce may be far more devastating and depressing than the death of a spouse.

A woman is depressed by shock to her self-esteem and the realization that she has been extremely dependent on her husband and her marital status. Now she flounders trying to get her feet on solid ground and learning to count on herself and make the many readjustments of a divorced woman. If a woman has to work outside the home she realizes how little worth a retired mother and divorced mother is on the job market.

So often when she is just on her feet there is a sudden remembrance from the past, such as a favorite restaurant, or a friend's unknowing remark about her husband. This depression is hard to fight because she must fight for her life and decide either to live with the destructiveness of bitterness and hate, or to get on with a new life. Often

I have seen women finally get on their feet and feel a self-confidence in themselves, very surprised at how much they have grown and how much stronger they have become as individuals.

A Physical Basis for Depression

We are now beginning to explore more thoroughly the possible physiological factors that can produce depression. Manic-depressive behavior appears to have a physical and interited etiology. There is a lack of the mineral lithium in a person, and when someone is in a manic state of behavior, then its administration can help prevent the depressed low. There are some side effects to using lithium that must be considered. It is not a cure-all for every depression.

As a person's body chemistry changes through aging or as a woman enters menopause, the hormone balance of the body chemistry is very important in preventing depression. The ability of the person to metabolize properly and utilize the vitamins and minerals necessary for health is now an exciting frontier in nutrition and biochemistry. There are exciting possibilities in the field of nutrition for a healthy body and mind.

The Advantages of Being Depressed

Some people have asked me that, if depression is so painful, why so many people hang onto it so tenaciously. The truth is that there are some advantages to being depressed. You would be surprised at how often a person's reply to my question, "Do you want to quit being depressed?" is simply, "I don't know."

The advantages of depression are many. It can be used

effectively to control a relationship. Depression allows a person the excuse of saying, "Don't expect too much from me. After all, I'm depressed. I can't do this or be expected to do that because of my terrible depression." It can provide a person with many valid excuses. When he thinks about life without depression he is confronted with living a responsible life. That can be frightening He can want to change but he is waiting until he feels like changing or feels better.

I am always asking a depressed person to start functioning and to start doing things that are positive. Remember, to do these things a person doesn't have to *feel like* doing them. A simple change in a day-to-day routine with good diet and exercise helps break the vicious trap of depression. A depressed housewife who cleans up her house even though she doesn't feel like doing it will feel a sense of pride and responsibility for her life. I am not afraid to ask people to do hard or difficult tasks. After all, it's doing the hard things that sometimes saves our lives.

Thoughts on Suicide

One of the taboo subjects for a long time has been suicide. Sometime ask a group of your friends what they think about suicide and people who attempt to and actually commit suicide. Responses to your questions will probably sound like these:

"A person who talks about committing suicide isn't serious but only wants sympathy."

"Suicide is a sign of weakness."

"People who commit suicide are insane at that particular time."

"Suicide is an unforgiveable sin in the eyes of God."
"Let's change the subject."

This is not a simple issue. Here are a few factors I use in evaluating the lethality of a person's suicidal communication to me:

1. Is there a history of chronic unhappiness and problems in that person's life?

2. Has there been a series of recent stressful events in his life that would tend to push a person to the breaking point? A report prepared for the March issue of the 1974 *Archives of General Psychiatry* tells of 53 people who had unsuccessfully attempted suicide to find out what situations preceded the attempts. The report found out that persons beset with more than three highly stress-filled events in the course of six months are more likely candidates for attempting suicide.

3. To whom can the person turn to for support and help? If he feels there is no one to turn to, then it is a serious matter. Suicide for that person could seem a logical method of solving his problems.

4. I would ask about the method of suicide contemplated. The lethality of suicide increases from a person planning to end his life with baby aspirin to a person who plans to use a gun, hang himself, or gas himself with carbon monoxide poisoning in his garage.

5. The sex of the person talking about suicide is another important variable. A male discussing it is three times the risk of a female talking about suicide.

6. I would also try to have the person tell me the purpose of his suicide. What is the message in this final act and for whom is it intended? Since people are am-

bivalent about life and death, I would naturally ask the person to wait one more night or one more day. If I can get him to hold out one more day, then the next day I may ask him to hold out one more day, then the next day I may ask him to practice jumping off curbs to see if he likes the sensation! Seriously, helping a person to wait can be the factor that turns the ambivalence of no to life to yes. I take seriously every person who talks about committing suicide. If no one takes a suicidal talk seriously, then a person might go to the extreme and do it just to prove his seriousness.

When I was working at a state hospital we had a teenage girl admitted who was suicidal. Some of the staff didn't believe her talk was serious until on an outing she jumped out of the car at about 45 miles per hour. In the months that followed she slowly began to make progress and in time was allowed to return home and graduate from high school with high honors.

On the night of her graduation, however, she went to pieces again and was readmitted to the hospital. When I saw her she was talking crazy talk so I got her to stop so I could understand what went wrong. Since she was a gifted poet I also asked her to start writing immediately of what she was experiencing. Since this was her first day back I reassured her that her stay would be a short one and she should begin to think about leaving the hospital the first of August. Somehow I had to communicate to her that I still believed in her and had great hope for a short stay.

During one of the counseling sessions we began to explore the three choices open to her: suicide, craziness and life. Suicide is such a final act. It's a person's last

message. I had her imagine jumping off the roof of a
hotel and what her final thoughts would be. What message
would she send to her parents? She thought for a few
minutes and then said, "The final message to my parents
would be that they never did listen to me or care about
me."

I stated that in human communications, the message
sent is not always the message received. How would her
parents receive or hear the message she sent in her final
act of suicide? She had not considered that aspect of her
message.

I suggested that perhaps even with this last desperate
communication they still wouldn't hear her. Instead they
might think, "How could you do this to your parents
after all we have done for you." They might also think,
"Well, what can you expect from a crazy daughter who
was in the state hospital." Then I asked what her message
to me would be.

She said, "See, even you couldn't help me."

I responded that if she decided to commit suicide I
couldn't stop her, nor could God. But I wouldn't feel
guilty but only very sad because she still could have
chosen life. "If you chose 'craziness' as a way of escap-
ing life, I would still hold you responsible for your
decision. But if you chose to sit and contemplate red
brick walls like you were doing the other day and drift
away in the recesses of your mind into those empty
corridors of nothingness, what would your message be?"

She replied, "See, you couldn't help me at all." I told
her she was right. If she chose craziness it was her
responsibility, not mine.

What followed was a long period of silence. She stared

at the floor and made no response so I waited; but I finally had to break the silence. "Where are you now and what are you thinking?"

Slowly she lifted up her eyes at me and said, "I'm very angry at you because you have destroyed all of my fantasies of suicide. You don't know how important these have been to me but now they are all gone. Now, what is left?"

I replied, "What is left for you is life." Her protest to that alternative was that life was hard and scary. I told her to name me anything of value that wasn't expensive or involved some risk. I asked if she wanted a cheap life and cheap love, or did she want something of value; something that would make her proud and that was worth believing in and fighting for, a meaningful life. Her answer was silence.

In the following weeks there was steady improvement. In early August she was to be discharged from the hospital. She came to see me for her last appointment, but her body posture was of a depressed person with a slow shuffle and eyes riveted to the floor. I told her that it was normal to be apprehensive about leaving the hospital, but her depressive routine wouldn't work with me. I told her I was sorry, but she flunked at being a patient. I checked with the ward clerks, nurses, and other doctors and they all agreed she had become a very bad patient and was detrimental to the morale of the staff.

I told her she was very bright and was thinking for herself. In fact, she was brighter than most people who worked at the hospital, and that was threatening. Furthermore, she was leading other patients to think for themselves. "You flunked, honey, as a patient. You can't come back here anymore because we can't allow people in this hospital who won't be good patients." She laughed and we gave each other a good-bye hug.

For several years at Christmas I would receive a card from her that would say, "It's hard and it's lonely, but I'm winning the struggle. I am still glad I chose life instead of suicide or craziness with its contemplation of brick walls."

Suicide can be a person's last hostile act and message. It can also be accidental, that of taking too many sleeping pills to get to sleep and being hit by the full impact of the pills that proves fatal. Suicide can be the result of lifelong programming that one day the person will commit suicide. Sometimes it is chosen as the way to put an end to all the turmoil in a life.

Most suicides are *not* the result of being "psychotic." People who are out of touch with reality are also at times suicidal and unable to make sound decisions about their life. Suicide is also used by the terminally ill person who seeks to end the misery and expense of an extended process of dying.

One of the most important aftermaths of suicide are the people who were important to the person who committed the act. Each person may wonder if he could have prevented it. It's not even uncommon for family members to feel a strong rage towards the person who ended his life. After the recognition of rage comes guilt for the rage and so is set in motion a vicious cycle.

I have suggested that if there is a great anger towards the person who committed suicide, one should finally say good-bye by writing all the thoughts and feelings he has toward the deceased in the form of a letter, or to role-play by talking to an empty chair as if the person were there.

In my understanding of suicide, a person has the right to choose death as well as choose life. There must come the realization that if a person decides to end his life, it is his decision. I do not feel that it is an unforgiveable sin in the eyes of God. God, as I understand Him, is far more loving and merciful and forgiving than we can ever conceive as human beings.

The most important thing to remember is that each of us has our breaking point because we are human, not just because we are weak. If we can learn to wait, the life we save may be our own.

HOW DO I DESTROY ME? LET ME COUNT THE WAYS

The quickest means by far are guns, a rope,
and an overdose of dope.
These ways are tried and true, thus I can
quickly snuff out the candle of life and hope.

The other ways are not as quick as sudden acts,
but I can destroy myself on the installment plan;
An hour, a day at a time can be my subtle but
effective death pact.
It begins when I feel too weary to care and I no
longer believe I can.

There are pleasant ways such as smoking and filling
my lungs with black tars.
To be sure, I cough and my voice does rasp, but I can
always stop before I take my last gasp.

The balm of alcohol does soothe my nerves and
numb my brain.
It does help my pain, but what is the gain.
Family fights, lost days, and perhaps in my car a

sudden crash of flesh and steel.
Then I will no longer feel.

My arteries and waist, bulging with fat from the
 good things I eat, French fries, pizza pies and
 tasty desserts
My poor heart pounds so hard to push the blood
 through all my fat, so I find it hard to physically
 exert,
But I eat and diet and diet and eat
 So in my life a thousand pounds to lose is no
 small feat.
My mother's words I hear repeat,
 "Clean your plate, millions have nothing to eat."

The hurts and insults of yesterday I dutifully record
 on the diary of my mind,
Thus I can always recall the time, the day and name
 of someone who was unkind.
The energy I use to keep the diary of my mind
 Prevents me from living with joy in the present time.

I have a rendezvous with success. I rush and
 frantically push my body to extreme distress.
These words echo in my mind—compete, compete,
 and never retreat,
 Strive for the best, so fast my heart does beat.
Be perfect, no less. Then one day I will have success.

But lost in the din is the voice within crying
 Stop! Be wise. Is this the life you prize?
A collection of things gathered while rushing to die
 but never finding out the 'why'.

How do I destroy me? I have counted a few of the
 ways.
 Must I always to destruction flee?

Can't I finally learn to be? To live now with no delay
   and even learn how to play?
Where do I begin?
   By listening to the voice within
To decide I want to change and stop the blaming game
   Then finally I can walk and not be lame.

The price I pay is not cheap
   but something of value is what I will reap.
I will begin with hope, reach out with love,
   Seeking to care and daring to give
So before I die I will finally live!

7

THE PROBLEM WITH DRUGS IS PEOPLE

Journey to a Far Country

I call on Karen Nelson to help me illustrate the changes from drug experimenter to weekend doper to hard-core addict. Her story is not an actual case study; but my fictitious Karen is, in essence, real. She is, in fact, a composite of many teenagers I've seen professionally.

She was a typical 15-year-old girl, 1967 vintage. She had cool, questing blue eyes. Her hair, blond and incredibly shining, hung about her shoulders as straight as if she had ironed it on the board—which indeed she's been known to do. She lived with her family in a beautiful suburban home complete with swimming pool, patio and barbecue grill.

Her father, Tom Nelson, was 45 years old, had become a $35,000-a-year success by virtue of hard work, good management and a degree in electrical engineering. He owned a company which manufactured complex electronic equipment for the aerospace industry. His wife,

Sue, Karen's mother, was 43, and a college graduate. She was attractive, kept in shape by swimming and playing tennis. She enjoyed being a parent, and enjoyed being valuable in the community.

Jim was Karen's older brother. He was 19, a freshman at a nearby university. He'd been an average student in high school until his junior year, when he seemed to find himself—even made the honor roll. He was quiet and ambitious, and wanted to become a lawyer.

Karen had usually made straight A's. She liked to paint, and she loved music—played the piano and had started guitar lessons. She had so many clothes, it was hard for her to decide each morning what she'd wear to school. Her dresses came from the best shops. She knew that she was beautiful and that she was the apple of her father's eye. Her parents knew that she was also a bit spoiled, and for that they cheerfully accepted the blame—for when did they ever deny her slightest whim?

Karen never lacked for friends or fun. She and her gang went on bicycle treks, splashed in their various swimming pools, gathered at the drive-in. She spent this summer with her grandparents in Ohio; she was eager to begin her sophomore year in high school.

She began the term on a note of wonder and curiosity. A new, secretive mood pervaded the students. They gathered in small groups and talked in undertones about dope—acid, grass, white crosses, reds. She couldn't believe her ears when her best friend, Pam, whom she hadn't seen since spring, bragged about vacation activities as strange as they were forbidden. Pam went to pot parties at the river, even dropped acid.

Karen was shocked, and Pam laughed at her. Said Pam,

"Don't knock it till you've tried it." She delighted in describing a trip on acid: "Everything was so *funny!* I could take a trip while I watched TV. Mom and Dad never caught on. They'd just say, 'You're sillier than Lucille Ball—and she gets paid for it.' "

In the weeks that followed, Karen read books about drugs. The books, along with her friends, whetted her curiosity. She wanted to venture, to experiment, maybe to smoke pot or try some pills. *But nothing hard. She just wanted to know what it was like to be high.*

Her chance came one weekend when her parents, invited out for cocktails and a dinner dance, allowed her to spend the night with Pam. Pam's room looked like a psychedelic poster shop: black lights, acid rock music, amplifiers, beads, and some huge cushions strung about the floor. Pam put on the latest Jimi Hendrix album; *Purple Haze* was her favorite song. She turned up the volume deafeningly, lighted up a marijuana joint, took a "deep hit," then showed Karen how to smoke. Karen had never smoked even an ordinary cigarette, so inhaling was a matter of coughs and sputters. Her throat hurt, too. But after several numbers, she finally got loaded. She felt so relaxed and the smallest thing made her laugh. Pot was wonderful! Whatever had she been afraid of?

It was several months later that Karen got a little bored with grass and tried some other drugs. School was still fun, and her grades were still mostly A's. Her parents never questioned when she'd go with the kids to the park after school, or when she spent weekends with Pam. Tom and Sue protested that their daughter played her records too loudly, assaulting nerves and eardrums. But they assured each other that brilliant, artistic, popular

Karen would never be involved with drugs. She had too much going for her!

It wasn't until Christmas that Karen first dropped acid. She was apprehensive; but she thought she knew what to expect because she had heard about all her friends' trips—their "mind-expanding" experiences. After that first trip, Karen felt guilty, but also proud because she'd been "where it's happening."

By now Karen began to be too seldom seen around home. Her mother complained that she spent too much time at Pam's house or messing around at the neighborhood shopping center. Sue would have been stunned if she had known that Karen was trying a variety of drugs: reds (barbiturates), white crosses (amphetamines), mescaline, LSD, and lots of grass. Funny, but she never had to buy any of the stuff. Her friends, bless them, were glad to turn her on for free. Karen believed she was handling drugs okay, and she was still firmly convinced that she would never, never shoot dope. After all, she'd been afraid of the needle since babyhood!

Looking back, Tom and Sue Nelson wondered why they hadn't worried about their daughter sooner. They did begin to worry when she seemed withdrawn and depressed more and more. When asked a simple question, or if she was mildly reproached, she might scream "Get off my back!" and storm out of the room, slamming the door. Was this just the normal rebellion of adolescence? They didn't know. But they were shocked at the report card Karen brought home at midpoint in the second semester. She had dropped at least one or two grade points in each subject.

Would discipline help? They tried grounding Karen

for a month after that bad report card, only to discover that she was sneaking out through her bedroom window at night to be with her friends. Then, one day, Sue searched her daughter's room and found a bottle of pills and plastic bag containing marijuana, and roll-your-own cigarette papers.

The shock was like a jolt of electricity. *Karen, our Karen, on drugs?* Confronted with the evidence, she denied guilt—said she was only holding the stuff for a friend. She became the picture of outraged innocence. How could her own mother and father suspect her! Had they no trust? And what kind of mother would invade her daughter's privacy like that?

Sue and Tom wanted desperately to believe their daughter. They could not accept the possibility that Karen was on drugs. They found it easier to accept the lie she told.

Anyone over thirty was a square. Being young, Karen and her friends knew where it was happening. They could laugh at speakers at the school's drug assemblies and at the corny movies designed to scare kids away from dope. When you are stoned, your head feels no pain. The thought of losing your mind or dying just doesn't apply to you.

Once, when Karen came home high on speed, she was animated and talkative. She inquired winsomely about Dad's day at work and admired her mother's hairdo. Two days later, she was sullen and insolent again, and Sue said, "Why can't you be like you were the other night? So sweet and outgoing like our old Karen."

Karen was finding out that when she was ripped on grass, school was a drag. The tensions between her and her parents became unbearable, the explosions more frequent. Tom and Sue were at wit's end. They knew by now that Karen was on dope. There had been too many lies, too many strange people. Matters went from bad to worse, and one night when Karen didn't come home at all, Tom and Sue gave her an ultimatum: She would stop using drugs, or she would get out.

So Karen, at age 16, was on the street. Was she a runaway, or a pushout? It doesn't matter. Now she had her freedom. No more family arguments—she could have a little peace and be with her friends. She hitched a ride south to Baseline Road, to a place called Earth House where there was always room for one more. Al and Jerry, the 20-year-old "landlords," welcomed her with open arms. They said she could stay as long as she liked; they needed an "old lady" to cook and clean.

In a short time, Karen's clothes looked like Salvation Army rejects. Her hair was dirty, she wore no makeup and her feet were thick with calluses from walking barefoot along the highway. It was there at Baseline Road that Al, a speed freak, tied off Karen's arm and shot a bolt of lightning into her veins. It was love at first rush; one shot of methadrine and all her problems were solved. Karen even wanted to change her name to Crystal, a nickname for speed.

The hangout at Baseline Road was no $50,000 mansion. It was an old farmhouse that had long ago lost the glass in its windows. It had no electricity or running water, but had a well and an old hand pump in the backyard, where there was a sagging privy.

Strange characters came for a night or a week and then moved on. The best room in the house was the living room, with a variety of chairs and sofas, and end tables for holding candles and kerosene lamps. The walls displayed a variety of decorations, from posters to a mural painted by an artist high on acid. Those same walls even boasted bullet holes, put there by a speed freak hallucinating an invasion of narcotic agents. Karen would never forget the odors—of desert dust, mold from spoiling food, stale cigarette butts, marijuana, sweat, urine; and the unmistakable odor of ether-based speed.

One of the hardest things for establishment-minded parents to comprehend is the compulsion of many of today's upper-middle-class youngsters to "escape materialism"—to go to a far country where they can experience poverty, dirt and communal sharing of food, love, sex and drugs.

Karen's "far country" was no more distant than a far-south road on the fringes of her home town, but her escape was exhilarating. She took the dirt and filth in stride, and gloried in looking after her new-found "family." The commune's accepted health diet became hers: grapefruit, pinto beans, brown rice, green chili, carrots, melons, honey on brown bread. This was independence! No one told her what to do!

One afternoon Karen and Al were walking along Baseline. The only signs of life were themselves and a dingy, lost-looking mongrel.

Suddenly the air was shattered by the roar of motorcycles bearing down on them. Karen waved. Motorcycle clubs were a familiar part of the scene and she recognized some of these riders.

But, to her astonishment, Al started to run. He was soon caught and imprisoned in a circle of riders with blood in their eyes. Why? Because Al had burned Whitey, one of the members, of $100. That was the amount Whitey gave Al to buy him some speed.

Al pleaded that he'd lost the money—a thin lie, because after he bought the $100 bag of speed, he took a little taste for himself and his friends, then forgot to stop until the stuff was all gone.

The next few minutes were filled with swinging bicycle chains and fists; and with Al's yells and moans as the enemy worked him over. The gang then turned on Karen and raped her repeatedly. Her screams ended when a fist smacked her into unconsciousness . . . .

She awoke at the farmhouse, where several of her friends were cooling her battered face with ice. Al was so badly beaten, it was a miracle that he was still alive. Both victims belonged in a hospital, but their friends had a fear that amounted to paranoia: a hospital represented law and order—the establishment. They might get busted if they showed up there with two mutilated, half-alive bodies.

Karen and Al slept on, literally "in the arms of Morpheus." In her drugged sleep, Karen thought she was home again, but the dream faded. She awoke to find she was still at the farmhouse, on a mattress soaked with sweat. She wondered how long she had been out, and was told, she'd been on morphine for five days. Al would be okay, except for some broken ribs, a fractured nose and a few missing teeth.

The summer was a blur of people arriving and departing, of highs and lows, of suffering through days when the temperature was 110° in the shade and the only way to be cool was to strip in the ditch. Nights were a time to be busy supporting her habit. She learned to forge prescriptions, to steal and deal. Disposing of stolen property became a competitive business.

Amazingly, Karen felt little or no guilt over breaking the law. When you take to dope, you take on a weird logic: anything is right if it gets you the fix you need. Even robbing a friend was right, and easy in at least one case, because she knew her way around Pam's house. That job was good for a stereo, a color-TV, a couple of diamond rings and a coin collection.

There was a limit to how long she could shoot speed without some relief from its certain results: paranoia, sleeplessness, malnutrition, dehydration and exhaustion. Inevitably, after four or five days on a speed run, Karen would turn to heroin. The heroin provided her with desperately needed sleep, let her start to eat and rebuilt her wasted body. The quiet euphoria of the junk made her feel good.

But heroin became the most cruel master of all. She went crazy waiting for the junk to come. She lived a life of 29-hour days and 10-day weeks. The obsessive fear of a bust built suspicion: was this alleged friend an undercover agent, or a snitch? Was there anyone she could trust? These anxieties plagued her mind constantly; so, like nearly all fiends, she carried a gun and a knife.

Hating her world, Karen was nonetheless bound to it. Her feelings of femininity had long vanished; in fact her only feelings were those provided by chemicals. By now she was very hard. She walked and talked like a dope fiend.

There is nothing glamorous about being an addict, but to remain one you'll lie, steal, betray your best friend.

Although the fear of arrest haunts you, it's an unreal fear, because you're sure you are different. You won't be busted; you are too clever; you don't make mistakes.

But then it happened. Policemen walked quietly up to the door of the farmhouse and knocked. Al opened the door, turned in terror to run. But it was too late. Al and Jerry went to the city jail; Karen, despite kicking and scratching, to the juvenile detention home. It was her birthday, her seventeenth.

The following morning, in a small, dark cubbyhole of a room, Tom and Sue Nelson saw their daughter. They stared at her in numb disbelief. This couldn't be their Karen—this creature wearing a matted mane of filthy hair and twitching as if something crawled under her skin. Karen's face was ashen, gashed with the open sores a speed freak gets from picking at his skin. Eyes dark-circled and bloodshot she looked more like seventy than seventeen.

Only one aspect seemed encouraging. Karen would promise anything if they'd take her back home.

At a court hearing her parents asked to take Karen home. Their request was granted, but first she must be medically examined and treated in the hospital. She had lost thirty pounds and her gums were inflamed. She was suffering from severe serum hepatitis caused by dirty needles used for shooting dope. She was, in short, a wreck physically and emotionally.

On Thanksgiving, roughly two years from the day Karen left home, Karen's family gave thanks for her return. But her parents and brother were edgy. How long would this remote stranger remain there? Karen herself felt like a stranger, but she wanted to stay.

For the first month she kept at home, resting, playing rock and writing to Al and Jerry in jail. She did go Christmas shopping with Sue, but the event brought no joy, no sense of belonging.

Her brother Jim, scoring honors in college, tried hard to understand Karen. They would talk for hours on end, and he came to realize how deeply she had been involved with drugs and crime. He was fascinated with her language and changing expressions—haunted, guarded, sly—as she talked about the drug world; he could see her change as she talked with someone on the phone.

Irresistibly Karen began to visit any of her recent companions who were still at large. "Just to say Hi," she assured her troubled parents. "You know I'll never shoot dope again—you think I'm crazy?" Ironically, there was a part of her that believed what she said—that she would go straight forevermore.

It was good to see her friends again and to smoke pot; but no needles, no speed, no junk. She was through with that scene. Yet in her purse she carried a silver spoon, blackened on the bottom—a souvenir of her misguided yesterdays. All she could think about was dope, the high she loved; and the thinking tore her with conflict and confusion.

Her parents persuaded her to get a job. The thought bugged Karen—of being trapped in one place for hours and having people tell her what to do. But through a friend of her father's she became a waitress in a hotel coffee shop. The work was not hard and the tips were good, but having to talk with straight people scared her.

Now and again one of her friends would drop in for a hamburger. "Hey, kid, you're getting fat. Here's some stuff to make you lose weight." Karen would say no: but her insides would churn and one night she dropped a tray of cups. She could hardly wait to get away, go to somebody's house and smoke up. But after three or four numbers she still wasn't high; grass was nothing like speed or junk.

The evening came when someone laid in her hand a packet of USP methadrine—righteous and pure. As if in a trance Karen got out her silver spoon and engaged in the ritual of fixing and shooting. *Your liver doesn't hurt anymore. One more time can't get you wasted. You don't have to work tomorrow, so celebrate!*

Of course she didn't stop with one hit. In fact, she lost count. She did not go home that night; she did remember—at 2 A.M.—to call and tell her parents she was staying with a girlfriend.

Tom and Sue knew in their guts what was happening, and it did not take long to confirm their fears. Beg and plead as they would, Karen quit her job within the week, left home again and lived with her dope dealer. Her behavior became self-destructive; she couldn't get wasted fast enough. Once in a while she would call Tom and Sue and assure them she was doing fine. They'd hear through friends that she was in Mexico, Laguna Beach or Berkeley.

Then, after two years had passed, Karen called home one day and cried, "Help me. I'm tired. I'm sick. I want to come back."

But the road back for Karen is long, tortuous and unpredictable. Her fate is in jeopardy. But miracles have happened. Perhaps one will happen for her.

Hippies—then drugs.

Now let's try to gain some understanding of the new drug culture which had spread across the land involving such a large number of our children.

Remember when there was a new prophet who chanted, "Turn on, tune in and drop out?" The "new religion" of Timothy Leary was based on a hallucinatory drug, LSD, or acid. This very powerful drug soon began to be the focal point of the psychedelic phenomena.

It was a time when music changed from the surfer beat and the folk music of protesting groups to an electronic cacophony of acid rock, psychedelic lights and wild, uninhibited dancing.

Clothing styles changed drastically with an emphasis on the bizarre, like a masquerade party. It was a time of beards and long hair, bearded and barefoot children, running away to San Francisco because there was going to be a love-in there. This whole new social movement burst upon the American scene from 1965 to 1967. The youth of our country were fascinated by and attracted to the hippies, the flower children with their love and peace symbol, and the psychedelic world of turning on with acid.

There wasn't a major magazine that did not have feature articles on LSD and the new "turned on" generation. In retrospect, I feel that in an eagerness to report, the media was very instrumental in the instant propagandizing of the psychedelic world.

LSD was featured as a wonder drug. It would open everyone's minds to a new awareness of self, heighten emotions and intensify the senses of color and beauty.

One could gain a new awareness of God, love and inner-peace. It was even thought to enhance creativity and help us understand the psychotic world of the mentally ill and thereby reduce the population of psychiatric hospitals.

In the spirit of flamboyant reporting many of our youth were drawn irresistibly to experiment with this new psychedelic drug and its world of experience. In fact, one wonders if the establishment wasn't one of the primary motivators for turning on the younger generation via its media of print and television. If you doubt this, read some major magazine articles during the rise of the acid phenomena.

Ironically, LSD was not the wonder drug it was reported to be, because it fulfilled none of its advertised claims. A person under the influence of LSD may subjectively feel that he is more creative, more living, more spiritual, but in actual behavioral change, one was not any of these things. Interestingly enough many of the great insights contributed to trips on acid could not be remembered; and if remembered, they did not change the person for the better.

Television was a major factor in spreading the philosophy and life style of the hippie movement which was first highlighted in the Haight-Ashbury area of San Francisco. Long-haired people with beards, strange poetry and unusual life styles were nothing new in the bay area. Beatniks had been doing their thing for years and didn't excite or entice the youth from all over the country.

It was only when the media reported and exploited the people of Haight Street and Golden Gate Park that it became a national phenomena. It struck a responsive note in the restlessness of youth who ran away in great numbers to the city.

The children came, the cameras came, and the tourists came to look at the freaks. It was a world of its own for a while with its own special kind of music, camaraderie, and newspaper.

Unfortunately there was also another side of the carnivallike atmosphere in San Francisco. That side was the tourists who were parents searching, showing photographs, and asking anyone who might know the whereabouts of a runaway son or daughter. These parents felt like foreigners as they wandered through the new hip scene and wondered if they would even recognize their child behind the new costume of the day.

For some the world of acid became a world of nightmares and insanity. The free clinic established in the Haight-Ashbury district became a psychiatric first-aid station for those entering the frightening world of toxic psychosis and overdose.

Other hard drugs such as methadrine, barbiturates and heroin made their appearance. With these harder drugs the world of love and peace began to change to a world filled with more violence and hatred. Instead of flowers being carried, it was now pistols. The original people knew that the hippie movement was dying. They held a funeral, duly recorded by the media, but the impact and the launching of a new youth culture centered around drugs was spreading as an insidious epidemic. There was a very real mystique to this culture. Adults didn't know what was happening.

The language sounded strange. There were words like: crystal, crink, turning on, tripping, spaced out, shooting, rushing, overamping, crashing, heads, highs, maintaining, bummers, sugar cubes, Owsley's acid, purple double domes, orange wedge, chocolate chip, yellow sunshine, rainbows, reds, yellow jackets, downers, pot, Acapulco Gold, Columbian Green, hashish, junk, smack, China white, blue endos, dropping, tracks, roaches, roach holders, STP, THC, mescaline, snitches, informers, busts, and narcs.

This new epidemic of drug abuse happened so quickly that parents, educators, politicians, police and health facilities were caught completely unprepared. The first major reaction was to deny the phenomenon and the dangers of the drug culture. Parents, schools, communities refused to see or recognize the problem, much less attempt to solve it.

I know that I was not prepared in my professional training or experience to know how to work with or begin to understand youth suddenly turning on to drugs. I remember when in September 1967, at a drug conference sponsored by the Arizona State Hospital, one of the featured speakers, Dr. Thomas Ungerlider, told us we should be prepared for an epidemic of drug abuse among our youth in Arizona. He described problems he was confronted with by drug users in Southern California, through his work at the UCLA Psychiatric Center. Typically, I think most of us felt it wouldn't happen in Arizona because we were different from those strange Californians. Arizona has long been known as a conservative state, both politically and in life-style.

But as Dr. Ungerlider spoke, the drug epidemic had already involved a large number of our youth during the summer months. When school started in September there was a whole new look in many of the young people going back to high school. The talk about trips last summer did not refer to family vacations.

The administrations in the high schools began to draw battle lines about dress codes and length of hair. The most vexing problem of all was what to do with kids using drugs on the campus. If a youth was arrested by the police, should the administration allow him to attend school? Being a known drug abuser, and especially being "busted" seemed to enhance his status among his peers. School administrations were afraid to admit publicly there were drugs on the campus because it would imply that the schools were a failure. For a long time the only admission that there was a drug problem was to have drug assemblies.

The next problem was to find drug experts in the community to talk to these "crazy" kids. Well, there really were no experts for this new drug craze. Policemen, lawyers, and doctors who had any information at all about drug abuse were called upon to lecture in assemblies. Drug-abuse films were shown, the great majority of which were inaccurate or overglamorized drugs themselves. Ironically, the kids knew more about drugs than the so-called experts.

I remember my first terrible experience when I was asked to speak on drugs at a high school assembly. At that time I was working with teenagers at a mental health clinic in Scottsdale, Arizona. I had talked to a few kids about drugs, but I knew next to nothing about drug abuse. I hurriedly read a book and gave a talk.

Worst of all, they had a question-and-answer period. How do you answer questions honestly without exposing too much of your ignorance? I remember one girl who asked, "What does STP stand for?" Well, I knew it was a powerful hallucinogenic drug, but I didn't know then what the initials stood for. But thanks to a sense of humor, I quickly answered, "Stop Teenage Pregnancies," and that got me off the hook. The kids thought I was real "cool." I later learned that STP stood for "Serenity, Tranquility, and Peace."

Soon psychiatric hospitals were being deluged with young people who had just been discovered taking drugs by their parents, or who had flipped out on acid; or who had been arrested and were hoping that being hospitalized would help their case in court.

During 1968 and through the summer of 1969 I continued to work at the mental health clinic with adolescents and at a private psychiatric hospital conducting group therapy for adolescents admitted there. The reason I mentioned this was the fact that the major portion of these youth were from better-class to affluent homes. It seemed the more luxurious the home, the higher the probability of drug abuse. This made the drug epidemic so hard to understand. Drugs had always been associated with the ghettos, the black and brown cultures, and not with "good" middle- or upper-class America.

To say that those of us who were working with these kids knew what we were doing would be a great distortion of the truth. If a young person was having a bad trip on acid, then a tranquilizer called thorazine would help terminate the trip and the hallucinations. But if the bad reaction was due to STP, the thorazine seemed to intensify and prolong an already frightening experience.

The very fact of giving medication to drug-abusers

seems somewhat incredible. Many young people said they were never so loaded as they were in the hospital from all the medication they had to take, in addition to the dope friends brought to them or they picked up on passes. It's hard to believe, but in rehabilitative therapy drug-abusers spent many hours making water pipes for smoking dope. Was this supposed to be therapeutic?

It was worth so many rungs on the status ladder if you could brag about how much dope you brought back from Berkeley or Los Angeles. To be a "groupie," and to have slept with many rock stars, was a big ego-builder for a girl. Names of big dealers in drugs were spoken of with a hushed reverence.

Very often it was the lonely kid who couldn't make it with his peers, who now had a magic passport to friendship. If this person could brag about how stoned he was, how he was busted or almost busted, all of a sudden he was *somebody*.

The first young people to turn onto drugs saw themselves as leaders of a new youth movement. This "now generation" was also a generation on the move, traveling across the country to rock festivals at Monterrey, concerts at the Fillmore in San Francisco, tripping with people on Haight Street or cruising the strip on Sunset.

It seemed that the psychedelic world of LSD and pot would make the youth a more together generation that rejected the plastic values of adults. In time a new culture developed with the beginnings of its own value system which were probably as influential in changing people's lives as the drugs themselves.

Parents Are People Too

Raising teenagers and being a teenager are not easy tasks today. The heated family arguments over the length of a son's hair or a daughter proclaiming her freedom by wearing no bra are seen as real threats to parental authority. Behind all the fuss concerning long hair and beards and bras is the very real fear of drugs.

So often parents talk about hair, when they really want to ask their son, "Are you using drugs?" Parents are also afraid of losing control over their children who appear to be listening to the beat of another drummer proclaiming a new life-style; a life-style with no morality, encouraging premarital sex and undermining family authority. It has no concept of the future because only the present, with its hedonistic pleasures, is to be enjoyed. Getting good grades in school and working hard are not part of the new life-style.

Parents are also aware and frightened that it's the affluent home, the "good" home, which seems to have more than its share of young people turning to drugs, taking part in demonstrations and blowing up buildings. Parents used to believe that as long as your kid's friends were from "good families" you need not worry about them too much. Unfortunately, good families may also have children who are using drugs.

It is soon quite obvious to parents today that you cannot rely on the way your parents raised you to be an adequate model for raising your own children. In fact even Dr. Spock's famous baby books didn't tell parents what to do when they discovered one of their children on drugs. Parents often feel very rejected by their children. Not only is their value system rejected, but they experience rejection as significant people in the lives of their children.

In a family therapy session a teenage boy attempted to defend his use of drugs by saying, "I don't see why I can't use dope as long as it doesn't hurt anyone else." As he spoke I observed the lines of worry, fear, and sadness etched in the faces of his parents.

I asked the boy to look at his parents and then I said, "Your parents are people too, and your doing dope is hurting them."

He replied, "It's my life. They shouldn't care what I do with it."

"Demanding that your parents not care about you is like demanding that the sun rise in the west instead of the east."

The common scapegoat for whatever ails children is traditionally the parents. This was made quite obvious by many TV dramas which tried to deal with the drug epidemic. It was all the parents fault. I won't deny that the American family and American marriage are faced with serious problems. The ever-climbing divorce rate is brutal evidence of the breakdown of American marriage. But, that failure doesn't explain the drastic escalation in drug abuse.

Drugs have claimed many victims, and many of those victims were parents. I have personally experienced the silent sorrow and grief of parents of drug abusers.

There are many parents who tell stories like the following:

"Our daughter is 15 and we don't know what to do as she is determined to kill herself. Twice in four days she has been brought back to life in the emergency room at the hospital. Where do you put a girl that is determined to kill herself with drugs?"

"Doc, do you know how it feels to go to work each day with a sick feeling deep inside your stomach because you can't stop your son from doing dope? Every time he came home loaded I wanted to smash him in the teeth but what good would that do? So I finally kicked him out of the house, and then my wife and I worry ourselves sick waiting up every night for him to come home. My wife is up three of four times a night checking his bedroom, looking out the window thinking she has heard him come home. Doc, it's rough. Your son is on the streets doing God knows what. Where will it all end? Did we do right in kicking him out? You know he is only 16."

"For over a year my husband posted bail, paid for lawyers, and all he got was an insolent attitude. My husband held his temper as long as he could but one night he finally blew up. It was awful, watching my husband and son fighting each other. Our son finally left."

"What do you do when you know your son set up your own house to be robbed? We lost our stereo, color TV and expensive jewelry; and he has the gall to still want to stay at home. We can't even kick him out. If we kick him out, he sneaks back in the window at night. He won't work and won't go to school. *He's* our son?"

"We've spent over $10,000 on psychiatric hospital bills, doctors and lawyers fees the past couple of years. Nothing seems to help. We tried to get him out of trouble, but there came the day when he was arrested, not for drugs but for forgery. What did we do wrong?"

There is also the very sad and sickening feeling of

standing by parents at the graveside of a daughter who died from an overdose. A beautiful, bright, talented girl —destroyed from drugs.

The first step a parent should take to become more understanding about drugs would be to look carefully in his own medicine cabinet to discover the amount of mind-altering drugs that are used, like prescriptions for diet pills, sleeping pills, pep pills, tranquilizers, pain killers. Then check the liquor cabinet. Try to evaluate your own use and abuse of chemicals and alcohol, remembering that the largest segment of our population using them is the over-thirty group. For years our culture has been successfully persuaded by pharmaceutical companies that relief is "just a swallow away."

For some reason, experiencing anxiety and pain is viewed as unnatural. Yet it is often through anxiety and pain that we become aware of problems that need to be faced and solved. Avoidance of pain through chemicals only dulls, not solves, problems.

The next step is to take time to listen to your teen-agers and have them educate you on the drug culture among their peers. Parents are often ignorant as to the powers of the peer culture in influencing adolescent behavior. Peers are often more important to the adolescent than his parents and this seems to be particularly true when it comes to experimenting with drugs.

Why are kids using drugs? The answer to the "why" are numerous and varied. Here are some of the reasons:

1) Drugs are taken because they have become an accepted fad in the youth culture, instead of swallowing gold fish or packing into phone booths. Unfortunately for many adolescents all they have heard about in the

last ten years is drugs, so they assume that kids have always turned on to dope.

2) People take drugs because of curiosity. If everyone is talking about drugs and drug experiences, then it is somewhat natural for a person to want to satisfy his curiosity about drugs by experimenting.

3) Drugs have become an expression of adolescent rebellion against parents and authorities. Dope is such an emotional thing with adults that many young people enjoy pushing the parental panic button by doing drugs, talking about drugs and then defying their parents to try to stop them.

4) People use drugs because they like being loaded or "high." A former addict said, "I loved the high of drugs, but I hated the addiction." Being loaded is fun, so why not do what is fun? People wouldn't do dope if they didn't like it. Drugs offer an instantaneous source of entertainment.

5) Drugs are taken for various psychological reasons. Drugs offer an escape from reality and a way to forget problems. Drugs are used to fill the empty void in a person's life. The troubled and inadequate person gets involved in drugs also to find acceptance and a chance to be somebody. Extensive use of drugs creates a whole new world of existence. Plans for the future are not necessary. Responsibilities can be forgotten. In fact there is a regression factor for some users to use drugs to try to recapture a previous time in their lives when there were not so many pressures and demands made upon them.

The emotional reactions of parents when they discover their children are using drugs are some of the following:

"What did I do that was wrong as a parent?" This is a reaction based on wanting to assume all the blame and guilt for an offspring using drugs. If a parent hangs onto the guilt and refuses to allow the person doing the drugs to accept the responsibility for his own behavior, it can lead to a very destructive process. It gives the parents a deep sense of gloom and depression and for the person using drugs a convenient mechanism to be used in manipulating the parents so he can avoid facing responsibility for his own actions.

"Why are you doing this to me?" This reaction is based on overpersonalizing the young person's doing drugs. In overreacting emotionally and seeing the drug-taking behavior as a plot to destroy them, the parents also fail to understand some of the other reasons for the person doing drugs. Some kids do drugs to hurt their parents, then others do drugs because they like being loaded. It is their decision and it is not always a plot to punish the parents.

This does not mean that knowing your children are experimenting or using drugs extensively is an easy thing to accept or an easy problem to solve, but it will not help the parent or drug user to come to grips with his problem if the parents overpersonalize the drug taking behavior.

Another reaction is to ignore all the clues, signs, and symptoms that a child of yours is using drugs. It is this defensive denial in which parents can't admit to themselves that their son or daughter is involved in drugs that allows the problem to grow and continue. It is always amazing when these parents can no longer deny the evidence (for instance, when a son or daughter is compelled suddenly to tell the truth, or is arrested for drugs, or else over-doses). Then they will admit that they have suspected the use of drugs by a son or daughter for at least a year or more, but they couldn't bring themselves to confront their precious child.

Parents may become suspicious. For instance, they find a letter addressed to a friend which describes in great detail the number of drugs he is using, how loaded he was, the times he used them and even his activities in selling drugs. However, the parents will deny the letter and say, "Oh, they are only bragging to impress their friends. I guess all kids talk about dope today."

The opposite reaction by parents in discovering that one of their children is on drugs is to explode in a violent rage and temper tantrum. There is either physical violence or the explosive impulse which results in throwing the young person out of the house and onto the streets. Kicking a son or daughter out for drugs may or may not be appropriate. It is never a good tactic when you first discover drug usage among one of your offspring. It is also a poor strategy when you first discover drug usage to call the police and have the son or daughter arrested and thrown in jail. There are times when all else has failed and in desperation a parent has to tell a chronic user to leave. This is always a drastic measure.

The best reaction comes from parents who have taken the time to educate themselves about drug abuse and have a good idea as to what facilities exist in the community for help.

The first thing that needs to be discovered is how serious the drug involvement is. Remember, that when confronted most users will lie as to the extent and length of their experimentation and use of drugs, but it is still important to forge ahead and gain some knowledge as to whether there has been experimentation for a few times, regular usage on weekends and if the person is shooting dope with a needle. It is a far different problem for a person who has smoked grass a few times than it is for a person who has been shooting dope. A person using a needle is a serious problem and needs outside help.

Remember, no parents should assume that their family is immune to the drug problem. If you have children, that fact alone should make you concerned. Before you become a super-sleuth or an amateur narcotic investigator, it would be well to remember that in dealing with adolescents you are dealing with a normally flaky person. Care must always be exercised in trying to distinguish, if possible, between normal adolescent behavior and adolescent behavior with drugs. For instance, one teenager told his mother after I gave a lecture on the danger signals of drugs and had mentioned lethargy as a sign, "Look, mom, I'm not on drugs. I'm just naturally lazy!"

The first indications to be concerned with are those of sudden and drastic changes in adolescent behavior. This includes extreme mood changes, changes in activities, interest and dress. For instance the adolescent who has been a good student is now failing, cutting many classes and ditching school, changes of interests from being active in sports and normal teenage activities to an adolescent who "puts down" and ridicules his former interests in life. These changes *may* have nothing to do with drugs but they should be investigated. Teenagers are normally moody people but an increase in extreme irritability or withdrawal should make you wonder what is going on.

The teenager who is spending more and more time away from home and gives very vague answers about where he has been and with whom he has been needs watching. You should be wary if there is an increase in secretiveness about telephone conversations and a feeling of intrigue as a teenager and his friends now talk in whispers hoping not to be overheard. If there is a sudden increase in telephone calls from people you have never heard of before, or a sudden increase in strangers coming to your home at odd hours of the day, you should be very concerned about the possibility of the adolescent being involved in the sales of drugs. Unexplained amounts of money when you know the amount of his allowance should make one very concerned.

One of the more serious indications of drug use is that of emotional apathy and lethargy, where now very little, if anything, interests the person. The adolescent who acts as if he is chronically depressed with no ambition or thought of the future and exhibits a deterioration in his personal hygiene and general appearance may be headed for serious problems. The extensive use of marijuana can produce a very lethargic and apathetic teenager.

Remember, there is a possibility that the adolescent is going through a normal growth spurt which may contribute to the lethargy and need for sleep.

How do you tell if your son or daughter is smoking pot? It looks like oregano and, when ignited, smells like burning alfalfa. It has a very pungent odor and will cling to clothes, furniture and the interior of an automobile. Marijuana smokers also like to drink wine because you can get loaded faster and stay loaded longer. Don't make the mistake of seeing your son or daughter stoned and then, finding out they have been drinking lots of wine, say to yourself, "Oh, he is only drunk again." The odor of marijuana is often covered by burning incense in the house. Since marijuana cigarettes are not commercially produced, you should be alert for the need for "roll your own" cigarette papers and strange clips called "roach holders" which now appear in the dresser drawer. After smoking marijuana a person is usually very hungry and sleepy with red and dilated eyes.

The user of barbiturates will often display a drunklike behavior without the alcohol. There will be slurred speech and a stumbling, staggering gait plus a need to fall asleep. Care must be exercised. If a person has had too many barbiturates a coma could be mistaken for a deep sleep that could result in a fatal overdose. When barbiturates are cooked up and injected with a needle they will often form abscesses like boils on the veins.

A user of amphetamines or "speed" will display various symptoms such as loss of weight, extensive sleeplessness, a constant need for water, a heightened sense of euphoria and well being, followed by a need for deep sleep (if a person has been shooting speed for several days), and then very depressed and irritable behavior. The most serious symptom is that of paranoia, which is the feeling that people are plotting against him, especially family and friends. This can result in emotional outbursts and violent behavior. A person who is shooting speed will also have widely dilated eyes and there will be the telltale puncture marks of the needle on his arms or the back of his hands.

The paraphernalia for someone shooting dope is a dead

giveaway. These include spoons that are blackened on the bottom, bloody cottons, candles, a hypodermic needle usually cut down, a syringe with a baby pacifier put on the end. There is also a belt, rope or necktie to tie off the arms to extend the blood vessels.

A user of psychedelic drugs such as LSD will often wear dark glasses because of the dilated eyes and a hypersensitivity to light. A person on a trip can often be hard to detect because dopers pride themselves on their ability to maintain around straight people; that is, to act as though nothing were wrong with them.

A person on acid can give you a wide variety of reactions, from very placid staring at an object for a long time, looking off into space as if he were living in a different dimension of time, or becoming very wild and frantic if he were experiencing a bad trip. If you discover that one of your children is on a trip resulting from a hallucinogenic drug, remember not to hassle, or get angry or frightened because it could cause a very bad trip. If you find that your offspring is having a bad experience from a psychedelic drug quietly talk to him and reassure him that everything will be all right. Then call a doctor or emergency treatment center for help. The talking down from a bad acid trip is best done when one is calm and reassured. After taking acid the user can become very exhausted and express a strong need for sleep.

It is very difficult to spot a beginning user of heroin or morphine. When a narcotic user is high his pupils may contract to pinpoints, he will display a drowsy, dreamlike behavior and he will be very passive. There can be a loss of appetite and constipation from the use of heroin.

The person's complexion also begins to take on a very pallid appearance. When a user develops a tolerance to heroin and is able to have a ready supply, he will act very normal and talk like any other person. Heroin can be either sniffed or shot into the veins with a needle. The person shooting dope will try to hide his tracks by wearing long-sleeved shirts.

When a user can't get enough junk he will begin to go through the classic withdrawal symptoms of extreme restlessness, sweating, nervousness, runny nose, nervous twitches, cramps, vomiting and diarrhea. It is at this time that the user is so desperate that he will do anything to get money for another fix. If parents are concerned about having a "junior junkie," they will suddenly discover missing items from the house which can be sold. Don't ignore this stealing behavior. A person using narcotics such as heroin and morphine needs help. The longer he shoots dope the more serious his problem with addiction will be.

In order to break down the walls of silence and shame, in February of 1970, I started a group called Parents Anonymous for parents with children on drugs. The first meeting at a local church was attended by approximately sixty parents, most of whom I knew because I had been working with their children and had visited them. Also, I extended a public invitation through television and the newspaper.

At first there was a nervous edginess in all those present, as if they were admitting to some great crime publicly. But soon one parent or another would recognize a friend or neighbor and they would greet each other with a "you, too!" attitude and in time people began to relax and discuss their problems. There were a million questions to answer and the parents had a great need to become educated about the drug culture and the various drugs that were being used.

The most positive aspect was that the parents seemed to give each other emotional support and no one felt alone anymore. To educate them there was literature, special speakers, films and most effective was the opportunity to talk to former drug users. It was a healthy experience to both the ex-drug-abuser and the parents to be able to build bridges of understanding.

I gave the major responsibility for organizing and maintaining Parents Anonymous to the parents themselves, and they were able to develop their own skills and strengths. A weekly meeting was called to order with a brief welcome and business session. Then the parents were divided into various small groups. There was a newcomers group where parents would stay for two or three weeks and be given a chance to ventilate their feelings.

Then the nature of Parents Anonymous was explained and the various sources for treatment was discussed. This also provided an immediate forum for their education in drugs. The other groups focused on parent-child relations, husband-wife relationships and personal confrontation.

The group leaders were volunteers who had experience conducting group therapy, through which people were able to grow and learn how to examine their own lives and become more realistic about their expectations for their children.

Parents Anonymous also developed a panic line for parents, a 24-hour answering service. Parents were trained on how to handle emergency calls by assessing the nature of the problem and having the knowledge of all the referral sources in the community.

Parents Anonymous has become a very successful self-help organization, not only in the field of drug abuse education, but has also provided many committed people to assist other drug programs in the city.

At a time when communication between parent and child, or adult and youth, is greatly needed, we are confronted with difficult barriers between generations. This barrier is not just the old "generation gap," but is an emotional barrier that has resulted in a widening or polarization between adults and youth, a polarization filled with distrust, anger, suspicion and paranoia.

The rage of adults is illustrated in James A. Michener's book on the Kent State killings when many parents felt that it was justified for the National Guardsmen to have shot the four students. Even when their own son or daughter was in the crowd the hatred was so intense that it didn't seem to make any difference who was killed.

The rage of youth has been vividly portrayed in the angry faces and the violent emotions of rioting youth. This polarizing into two paranoid worlds presents a real threat to the survival of our nation.

Let's take a look at the generation gap. First of all it is very important that there is a generation boundary between adults and youth. When parents don't maintain that boundary it can produce a very confused relationship with a son or daughter. No teenage daughter is overjoyed wtih a mini-skirted mom who is trying to compete with her friends.

The real generation gap existed in the early part of

this century when the United States was being populated by immigrants. Families had serious problems when the children wanted to speak that foreign language called English, eat new foods called hamburgers and apple pie while the parents doggedly held on to the customs and language of the old country.

The communications skills in the family today reveal serious interpersonal problems. Husbands and wives often complain that they cannot communicate satisfactorily with each other. Remember the husband who said, "The other night when our TV set was broken, I talked to my wife."

By the time a family has teenagers, mother has usually been the one who has been most involved in raising the children even if she has an outside job. The husband and father has spent more of his energy in his work and doesn't play as important a role in the family structure. This is very true in the higher-income business and professional families where the father has been a very unknown quantity until mother became uneasy about raising the teenager. Especially if the adolescent was discovered using drugs, the rather mysterious figure called father then tried his hand at being the authority figure in the family. He discovered how difficult it was to talk to the teenager he really didn't know. As a result, his fireside chats became long monologues filled with a demand for respect, which is as difficult as demanding that a person "be spontaneous."

When there is a problem with a teenager it brings into focus the real communication problem within the family. There is a realization of how little some parents know about their children, their children's friends or their world. The most important strategy for a parent should be to find ways to open the channels of communication with their children by listening more than talking.

Listening sounds very easy, but in reality it is a difficult art to achieve. A teenage son or daughter often tries to shock the parent and test the relationship to see how safe it is to be open and honest. If a parent can listen without interrupting, without a sermon, name calling or mind reading, that parent will learn a great deal about his son or daughter and the world of youth. It is very hard to listen without wanting to answer back right away or without planning the next reply. Just concentrate on trying to capture the experience of the world of the communicator.

Let's talk about the view of the different family structures and relationships which can produce difficulties with children.

Extremely overpermissive parents are too often parents who do not set adequate guidelines for their children and who try too hard to be good parents. They view children as miniature adults and too often give them the kind of love which does not differentiate between good and bad behavior. Whatever the child does is great because it is their son or daughter.

I will never forget a college-age youth who was seriously involved in drug abuse. He had been arrested for dealing drugs, kicked out of the University and hospitalized for emotional difficulties in a psychiatric hospital. He called his father who lived out of state to break the news of all his troubles. After he hung up, the youth was just furious with his father's lack of reaction. He said, "I wish just once my father wouldn't be so damned understanding and would just react and get mad."

Often what passes as a very permissive, modern parent is really only a parent who is indifferent to the children and who really can't be bothered with what happens to them. It is much easier to always say yes to avoid a hassle and slip the kid some money so he won't bug you. The child experiences this indifference for what it really is—rejection.

It is true that some parents are just frightened of teenagers, even their own. Our society has become so child centered that parents often feel threatened by the supposed power and force of teenagers. Their children find it easy to use emotional blackmail to get away with anything. The kids know that the parents are afraid of them, afraid to say no to them, or if they deliver an ultimatum they know their parents will back down and not carry it through.

The overrigid and overauthoritarian parent can also be just as disastrous. The authoritarian is always demanding respect, telling the children every move to make and then criticizing his children for not assuming more responsibility for their actions. This kind of family leads to a very disastrous power struggle between parents and children. Unfortunately, the children who are caught up in this power struggle use rebellion and negativism as a sole basis for their behavior. All they can do is react.

A teenager once described his lifelong power struggle for him to get good grades by saying, "My parents can take away my car, ground me, cut off my allowance, but they can't take away my F's. I can still flunk!" Because of the negative power struggle the adolescent feels that nothing he does is ever right. All he hears is how wrong he is and what a disappointment he is to the family.

How do you become a more adequate functional family? This topic goes far beyond the bounds of this book. However, there are a few guidelines that I feel are important. First, don't be afraid to be a parent and, while being a parent, try to remember the turmoil of your own adolescence and how you reacted and acted out against your parents and society.

Having family interactions more truthful and open can be a very positive step. The problems of trust and honesty become paramount when parents find out that their teenager has been lying and using drugs. Now the family is faced with the very difficult task of building trust and faith again. The adolescent who has trained his parents not to believe in him and to see him as an untrustworthy person will have to face realistically that it will take some time to build up a trusting relationship.

Very important in solving family problems is the concept of being reasonable. If families can negotiate various requests under the terms of whether it is reasonable or not, then there can be some honest give and take.

What about discipline? Basically discipline is a process of learning, not punishment. When a young person has really blown it, I think it's time to set up some guidelines for discipline. This means that the youth realizes that discipline will give him some time to remember his stupidity; that he can do some hard things so he'll remember and learn from the experience; and learn there are consequences to his behavior.

It has been enjoyable to see families engage in the process of working out discipline with the offender present. First a length of time is decided upon, and then some things to do are outlined, which range from picking up tin cans along the highway on weekends to digging ditches or scrubbing the kitchen floor with a toothbrush.

The reason that this concept of discipline is important is that it provides immediate feedback for unacceptable behavior. I have seen too many youths who repeatedly got into one jam after another with the law or with the family, and then discovered that nothing ever happened. This resulted in the youth feeling a sense of omnipotence that he was above all the laws and he could always get out of the trouble he made for himself.

Unfortunately, if the antisocial behavior continued there inevitably came a time when there was no way for the person to get out of the consequences of his behavior and this resulted in his incarceration in reform school, jail or prison. There are times when it is beneficial not to bail a son or daughter out of jail ten minutes after they have been booked. Now please don't think I believe that sending people to jail is the answer, because I don't. But sometimes when a person is just getting started in criminal behavior he needs to get a taste of the consequences of his behavior before it is too late.

One of the hardest things to accept for any parent is his inability to control all of the behavior of his teenage children. It is hard to accept the important fact that children must make their own decisions, good or bad, regarding their lives. Parents can't control their children's thoughts and feelings, their lives or destinies.

This means that we begin to accept the retirement process from the role of being a parent. It seems strange that there have been thousands of books written and every woman's magazine has an article on how to be a parent,

but no one has written a book on how to retire from
being a parent. Retiring from the role of a parent means
letting go of your children and redefining the relationship
to one of equality; of adult-to-adult and not parent-to-
child.

After all the years of being the child's guidance-coun-
selor, advice-giver and decision-maker, it's hard to say,
"It's your life. Make your own decisions!" There comes
that day when a parent realizes there isn't any more he
can do for his son or daughter except to let him go on
his own. This is especially difficult for parents when their
child is of age, is still using drugs and refusing to change.

The only alternative left is to emotionally cut him loose
with the message, "It's your life now. Whether you continue using drugs is your decision. Whether you go to
jail or die is up to you. As your parent I can't do any
more, and furthermore I don't want to watch your slow
destruction before my eyes, so please leave. Go out and
shoot your dope. I can't help you."

This means cutting the son or daughter loose knowing
full well that they will have to hit bottom, and there is
no magical cure in hitting bottom. Some sink so low
they have to reach up to touch bottom. Some die. Some
go to prison. And some decide there must be a better
way to live.

The problem with drugs is people. I discovered the
only way I could talk about drug culture was to describe
it in terms of four variables. (1) The personality of the
user, (2) the purpose of the drug use, (3) the potency
of the drug, and (4) the people the drug user associated
with.

Personality of the User.

Let's take a look at the personality, an extremely important variable. The use of drugs, such as smoking pot, will be far different for a 13-year-old than for an older person. Maybe the best way for me to illustrate the personality variable is to have you picture four people in a room smoking pot from the same lid and to explain some of the varieties of the reactions due to the personality and past experience of each user.

The first one is an experienced pothead. He just loves to get loaded and spends most of his time getting high. He takes a deep hit on a joint and passes it on to the next person in the room who is there for the first time to try marijuana. The next one takes a deep hit, coughs a lot and passes it on to the next person. This one used to be on psychedelics until he flipped out on acid and spent many months in the state hospital trying to get his head together. He has vowed he would never again take any heavy hallucinatory drugs for fear of that recurring experience, but he believes that he can still smoke pot.

The last person in the room is a former speed freak who had shot a great deal of methadrine into his veins. He said methadrine was like falling in love with a very beautiful, voluptuous woman you know will destroy you. This speed freak had gone crazy for a time with a toxic psychosis of paranoia and had decided to quit, after losing lots of weight and going crazy; after having a damaged liver from hepatitis from using dirty needles and fighting the deep depressions when he would crash after shooting speed for many days with no sleep and little food. He decided he had found the cure for speed. It was called heroin. He was finally arrested and, after doing some time in jail, decided to never put a needle in his arm again. But what harm could come from smoking a little pot?

As the evening proceeds and more marijuana is smoked, the pothead gets stoned and feels very relaxed. The first-time beginner is still coughing and wondering if he was stoned yet. The former psychedelic user is beginning to become very anxious, paranoid and panicky. He's beginning to recall some of the old nightmares when he flipped out and ended up in the psycho ward at the county hospital.

The former speed freak is trying to get as high as he did on methadrine, but he can't. What has happened to him is that he has pushed the "on" button and now all the old tapes when he was in the world of speed and junk are coming back into his awareness, and he's trying to reach the high of speed while smoking marijuana. In essence he is smoking grass, but thinking about the rush of speed. There's a very good chance that he will soon be tying off his arm and cooking up a spoon of speed, and will then be again caught in the destructiveness of shooting dope.

Purpose of Drug Use

The psychological state of being varies with everyone. The twelve-year-old and the thirty-year-old are different. The purpose of using drugs is also different. Many young people experiment with smoking a little marijuana and say, "Big deal! So that's all there is to it. Well, at least I've tried it. So that makes me cool." I call this one a level one drug experimenter, one which most drug users are. They try it for a while and quit. The second level drug user is one who spends his or her weekends getting stoned and usually will try a variety of drugs like mixing wine with grass, barbiturates, white cross, and amphetamines; and maybe some hallucinatory drugs. This person is close to trouble with drugs, because he or she can begin now to smoke pot before school or at lunch and never quite make it back to class after lunch.

If the person becomes a level three user, like Karen, he or she then uses drugs as a way of life, 24 hours a day. Being stoned is the most important goal in life.

I have worked with many young people who have smoked lots of marijuana each day for about three years, and what I see in them is very pathetic. Often a young person has been a very bright student interested in many activities. But now he is very lethargic, chronically depressed, and is giving evidence of neurological brain damage. He has no goals or ambition but to get stoned.

A person in this position occasionally has a spark of life and says, "Wow, man, some day I might go back to school or get a good job." He and his friends are so impressed with the thought of doing something positive with his life, that everyone says "Man, this is heavy," but the spark is soon gone. However, the person actually feels like he has accomplished something, just because he thought of doing something, someday, with his life. Now he is relieved of the burden of actually doing something about it for a while.

I will never forget a young man who said to me, "Doc, you know how all the experts say that marijuana is harmless. (By the way, experts today are no longer sayir that it is so harmless). Well, if it's so harmless, it sure made me lazy! Like, man, I was stoned for three years and have an eighth grade education. Now I'm seventeen and have quit, but what can I tell a prospective employer what I did with those three years? Oh, man, can I just say that I was bombed for three years? Maybe that's why they call it dope, because I sure was one."

I did work out a plan for him to get help so he could get his high school diploma, but he had lost three years of his life.

One day I was discussing the first Woodstock with a drug user, about how the media and the public had been impressed because there had been no violence. His analysis of Woodstock really blew my mind. He said, "Doc, you could look at it this way. Woodstock was a frightening experience because it showed how you could put hundreds of thousands of people in a concentration camp and you wouldn't even need any fences or guards. You just needed to give them lots of dope and loud music and that's all. Look at all those people in the mud and rain, with not enough toilets or food. They were just numb people feeling no pain. It scares you when you look at it that way, doesn't it, Doc?"

Potency of the Drug

The third variable is the potency of the drug that is used. One of the major difficulties in doing valid research on marijuana is that the potency varies so much from climate to climate. For instance, something that is growing wild in prairies in the midwest is far different from the marijuana grown in South America or Africa. There is quite a big difference between the potency of one joint of marijuana and a little resin of hashish. Even though hashish is made of marijuana, it's 25 to 50 times as potent. Any time you buy or are given street drugs, you never can tell whether you are getting baking soda or strychnine or whether the mescaline is really mescaline or somebody's LSD or STP they can't get rid of. The paper of heroin you buy could only be 2 percent or 100 percent. One doesn't do much, and the other cures your heroin addiction because its side effect is rigor mortis.

Associates of the Drug User

The fourth variable is the people variable. The people one associates with in the drug culture are very important. Marijuana doesn't lead a person to use heroin, people do. For example if a young person associates with a group of friends who occasionally smoke marijuana, there is very little chance of that person going to harder drugs.

It's a far different story if the young person begins to hang around people who are using a variety of hard drugs, barbiturates, speed and heroin. If a person stays with the group, "a friend" will help him to a new and better high. After all, he gets tired of one high and has to go on to the next. Too long we have approached the problem and solution as a medical-chemical problem. We haven't paid enough attention to the real problem which is psychological.

For example, in the history of this country, there was once a great problem with morphine addiction. Then a new wonder drug was invented to cure morphine—it was called heroin. We then had a bigger problem—heroin addiction. Now we have invented another wonder drug called methadone. Maybe the death rate due to heroin overdose is decreasing, only because the addicts are dying from methadone overdosing; or using methadone with liquor or barbiturates and then dying.

You can lock up a junkie for five years in a prison. His body has no craving for heroin, but all the time he is behind bars he and his fellow junkies think and talk about shooting dope; copping dope and forging prescriptions; how to improve as a burglar and as a robber. Twenty-four hours after being released from prison, the junkie will already have scored and rewarded himself with heroin.

A very interesting phenomenon in the drug culture is a very warped sense of values. Do you realize that most drug users do not consider the crimes they commit to get their dope and the act of using it as criminal behavior? And yet heroin addicts are the main reason for the crime rate in our major cities.

You also know that many of the dealers who bring in large quantities of drugs from foreign countries are not of the Mafia or of some organized international criminal syndicate. There are many young people from nice homes who say they are working their way through college and are just getting a little practice in business—the drug business. They are quite indignant when they are caught and confronted with their felonious behavior.

I am not going to minimize the fact that the greatest part of our drug traffic is through organized syndicated crime. The reason why it is such a big business is that there are billions of dollars to be made in illicit drugs.

Some countries have taken rather drastic measures in

trying to solve the drug problem. Some have made it a capital offense to sell drugs. That sounds very harsh even to think of as an alternative, and yet at times I wonder if we will have to go to that extreme; that the person dealing in quantities of drugs will be apprehended, brought to a speedy trial and then executed.

A car thief admits that he's a car thief, but a person using drugs does not believe he is a criminal.

I don't want anyone to get upset, but I do believe that people caught with marijuana in their possession for the first time should be charged with a misdemeanor.

The power of the drug culture, with its self-centered appeal, and the apparent ease with which it accepts a lonely teenager, can soon do a very thorough job of brainwashing that person into a different life-style. "It's your life, so do with it as you please so long as you don't hurt anyone else." The only time that philosophy works is if you are on an island and you are the only person there.

If I were to run a residential center for addicts, I would first insist that if a person wanted to save his life he would have to begin by changing his outward appearance. He would have his hair styled. Beards would go. He would wear new clothes like straight people wear. Music —but not acid rock—lots of other kinds of music; many books to read. Talents would be developed that have never been used, but forgotten long ago. Thus when a person got his thinking squared away and left the treatment center, he would be so different in his outward appearance that a person from the drug culture would look at him and wouldn't want to have anything to do with such a straight-looking person. It would be a way of keeping him away from the drug culture.

A person who has been on hard drugs cannot afford the luxury of going around to see old friends and visit old haunts. If he stays around too long, he'll end up right back where he started, at the bottom of nothingness.

Someone addicted to speed or heroin should realize they cannot substitute alcohol for speed or heroin. He can just as easily become addicted to alcohol and have trouble. And once using and abusing alcohol he will begin to think about heroin because alcohol and heroin are downers, and heroin has no hangover. He won't have a hangover as long as the heroin supply lasts, and he'll feel no pain. Someday he'll have nothing to worry about, never have to feel pain!

The magnitude of the drug problem in this country and throughout the world is even more staggering when you realize that alcohol is the number one drug problem among all ages. Please, parents, don't be happy that your teenager is coming home drunk and say, "Oh, he's only been drinking. I thought for a while he was on drugs."

Somehow we've gotten the philosophy that there is better living through chemistry of the mind. Billions of barbiturates, amphetamines, painkillers and tranquillizers are consumed in the routine practice of medicine in the United States. Then we wonder why we have a drug culture and a drug-oriented way of solving problems!

This is supposed to be a book about a psychology of hope! And up to this point, this chapter has been bad news. Well, as they say, I've got some good news and some bad news . . . Now, here's the good news, and some signs of hope.

First of all, I feel that the medical profession itself

realizes its responsibility for writing prescriptions for drugs like amphetamines. Amphetamines have about one bona fide use and that is for sleeping sickness. They do not work in losing weight—this is a proven fact. They will drive people crazy—this is a proven fact.

We used to think that barbiturates would help us sleep better, and now studies are showing that barbiturates do not give us the restful sleep that we need . . . and tranquillizers have not been the promised wonderland. Now some tranquillizers have helped people with hallucinations—but we still have to find ways for people to change.

We have a large number of people who are prescription drug addicts. Sometimes it's the everyday housewife who is on a very vicious cycle of going to as many as five doctors getting prescriptions for librium, valium or milltown. Then she uses alcohol in the afternoon after dexadrine has gotten to her nervous system a little too much. She takes a seconal at night to sleep.

Doctors are beginning to watch this very carefully now, and realize that care must be given in what they prescribe. Many physicians said the first thing they did was alter their habits in prescribing mind-altering drugs. Also there is no great enthusiasm for abuse of psychedelic drugs. The use of methadrine is definitely down.

More important I am seeing a change in young people. They saw what drugs were doing either to themselves or to their friends, and were educated firsthand. They have made some decisions about their lives. We are seeing a new type of young person today who is interested in meditation, who is coming back to religion and is far more serious about his life and his goals, and the quality of life he wants to have around him.

If you ever want to know what young people are thinking, I heartily encourage you to listen to their music. We are hearing some very beautiful music today. We are finding that young people are showing a trend toward more natural fun. It's a good sign and a ray of hope to see the youth of our country enjoying life and able to have fun without chemicals.

Maybe when we realize that part of the problem has been that as families we have broken down. In our rush for instant happiness we found just the opposite. Now we are finally getting back to getting our own values straightened around. We are realizing our priorities and find what really counts is people. When you let people know that they count, especially the young people in your family, and you listen to them, then there is real hope.

8

I'M NOT CRIPPLED.
I JUST DON'T WALK VERY WELL

One of the most beautiful persons I have ever met was a woman who had a home not far from my office. I met her when I was asked to evaluate a young child who had been abused by her mother, and had been placed in a foster home. By my book this foster mother should be acclaimed "Citizen of the Year." Into her home she welcomed as many as nine unwanted children who were crippled, mentally retarded, or otherwise disadvantaged for physical as well as emotional reasons. I'm sure in her heart are emblazoned the words, "Suffer the little children to come unto me."

In my discussion with her I was overwhelmed by her love, her patience and wisdom. I asked her to describe how she handled the many different problems brought to her by the children who nobody else really wanted. She told me of a black girl who had been with her for a number of years, and who had been crippled by polio.

No one wanted to adopt her or to take in a foster child who was black and handicapped. Instead of allowing self-pity to be the dominant emotion, she taught this young girl to accept her limitations and not feel sorry for herself. When someone asked her how it felt to be crippled, she was taught to reply, "I'm not crippled. I just don't walk very well." Doesn't that just startle your mind!

People can also have a way of bringing me back to reality and bringing me down on my knees. In the state hospital once I had a 28-year-old woman assigned to my therapy group. I must confess that at first I was very annoyed and bewildered with what to do with Anna because all she could do was mumble and cry. As soon as the group was over I got her chart from the files to find out why they had put her in my group. She could hardly communicate at all beyond undistinguishable sounds. As I read her chart, I felt very ashamed.

Anna had been in a terrible automobile accident on Okinawa last summer. Her father, mother and fiance had been killed instantly. Her face had gone through the windshield and she had been in a coma for at least two months. She was now suffering the aftereffects of brain damage and depression. The chart went on to say that Anna spoke Chinese, Japanese, Spanish, French and English fluently. She was a professional pianist, a geisha, entertainer and teacher in a special education school. In short, she had more talent in her little finger than I had in my whole body, and here I was, complaining about her being in my therapy!

Through the weeks that followed, I was able to sense that she felt guilty about still being alive when the others had been killed. Ever so gradually her depression began to lift, and I saw her reach out to others in the group and give them hope and encouragement. She tried harder and harder to speak with more clarity.

One day when I came to the hospital to conduct the group a nurse asked to speak to me. She said, "Anna has given up on life and has decided to die. She won't eat and she won't get out of bed. Would you please go see her?"

So I went into Anna's room and said, "I hear you want to die?" She nodded her head. "Anna, I also know a secret. It's that part of you wants to live also."

She smiled and said, "How did you know?"

"Oh, I think in the months that we have known each other, I have gained a little insight into you. Let's take stock of your life right now. First you have made enough improvement to be aware of what you have lost in the accident. You have been an extremely talented, bright, vivacious person." I listed all of her talents. "To become aware that you may never play a piano again or dance or teach or speak fluently is an incredibly hard reality to face. The automobile accident has taken away many of your talents and gifts, but in the months that I have seen you in group, I realize that your greatest gift was not damaged in the accident, that of a loving heart. I have seen time and time again your loving and caring for people. Now don't you think it's time to come to terms with your limitations, and get on with the living. Not everyone, Anna, has the gift of a loving heart." As she smiled and nodded, I went on to say, "I'm not a neurologist and don't know how much improvement can be made because of the brain damage, but let's see how far we can go to gain back what the accident hasn't taken away. Maybe if the medicine can be reduced, you can concentrate and practice walking better so you won't just be falling into the walls. There's an old piano in the ward, so perhaps you can start playing again. We don't care what it sounds like, but we just want to see what can come back."

So together we outlined a strategy for her recovery. Anna amazed everyone, including herself. When she heard someone in the group begin a self-pity trip, she would quietly say, "Don't you think you need to come to terms with life and your limitations, so you can get on with your living?" Well, when Anna spoke out of her loving heart, knowing what she had experienced, you had to listen.

That summer Anna was discharged from the hospital and went back to Okinawa. She was still handicapped, but was still able to love and to work as a teacher's aide in special education.

Some of you reading this have physical handicaps. Maybe you're thinking I make it sound so easy to come to terms with one's limitations. It isn't easy, believe me, because the normal path to take is one of bitterness and self-pity. We become discouraged so easily that we quit trying and give up hope. We surrender to the feeling that no one in the world really understands how it is to be handicapped.

Parents are often confused and baffled as to how to treat a child with a physical or mental handicap. One of the hardest steps for parents of handicapped children to accomplish mentally is that final acceptance that a child of theirs is emotionally or physically handicapped. They are overprotective and feel personally guilty, and that they must somehow make it up to the child because of the handicap life has dealt him. There is a myriad of emotions that manage to blur a parent's thinking. Too often a mother becomes so emotionally involved with a handicapped child that it almost consumes her at the expense of her relationship with her husband, and the rest of her family suffers as well. She pays the price by losing her own identity as a separate person. This doesn't help the handicapped child grow, but interferes with his becoming as self-reliant as possible. The heartaches that the handicapped child suffers are also compounded by the cruelty of other children in school.

I once had as a patient a very pretty thirteen-year-old girl with one leg that was shorter than the other. At birth an infection had destroyed her hip socket. She was depressed because the kids kept teasing her and called her names like "Crip," "Limpy" and "Gimpy." They always asked her why one leg was shorter than the other. She asked me what she could say back to the kids.

"Well, first of all," I said, "we must come to terms with some of the facts of life. First of all, you can't have a new hip socket put in until you finish growing. What we have to deal with are your feelings about yourself and how you let the other kids tease and push your "on" button when they ask you why one leg is shorter than the other. Next time just look them straight in the eye, and tell them you were born on a steep mountain, that's why." When I saw her laugh, I knew she could break up the negative tape of self-pity, and would not always be waiting for the next remark to hurt her.

Then she said, "Well, Doc, there is one very mean boy who's always bugging me about my leg and he won't let me alone. Is there something else I can say to him?"

"Well, the next time he asks you, you say, 'All right, I'm going to tell you the truth. One time there was a boy almost as obnoxious as you. Finally one day he made me really mad. I kicked him in the butt so hard that it shoved my leg bone right through my socket. I've about had it with you. I'm thinking about making my legs even by doing the same with my left leg so you'd better grab your ankles!" She liked that, and was able to hang loose instead of being so depressed.

I once told that story on a radio talk show and talked to a woman who called in on the phone. She said, "For years I had a problem with my hands being very shaky. I became so self-conscious that I wanted to avoid people who always asked me why my hands were shaking. One day a friend heard about my problem and said, 'The next time somebody asks you why your hands shake, just tell them that they don't shake. You just move quickly!' Well, I laughed! You are certainly right. My laughter set me free from the fear of other people's prying questions and my own self-consciousness."

There is an old spiritual whose title is *Nobody Knows the Trouble I've Seen,* which reminds me of a family I knew in California. In 1954 I was called to Canoga Park to start a Lutheran church. Starting a new congregation from scratch is a great challenge, especially when the whole congregation could walk down Main Street under one umbrella—Jeanne, our son Mike and myself.

There is no other way to start, but to walk door-to-door inviting people to be a part of the new congregation. Here's where my training as a salesman for Watkins products in Minneapolis had been such a good preparation for me!

It was summer, and one of the doorbells I rang was at the DeMars home. The woman who answered the door was named Hilda and gave me a warm welcome. True to her nature, she asked me if there was something she could do for me, perhaps give me a cold glass of milk or water. It was quite evident that there was a house full of children. I asked how many, and Hilda said, "We have nine children. We're very thankful to have all of them alive, because six of them had had polio in one year."

This seemed absolutely incredible to me, and as I grew to know and love each member of the family, I realized what a privilege it was to know them. Hilda's great love for her husband and for her children—in fact for the people of the world—was something you experienced immediately, as if it radiated from her skin. She never complained and always wanted to be doing one more thing for somebody else. Their home was, at times, filled with stray children; lonely children who wanted to be there and touch a little of the love in the DeMars home.

Their father, Don, was a really big man. I'm not exactly small myself, but he was tremendous! He spoke in a deep, deep voice with a rasping quality. Even when he said "Hello," you felt like answering, "Yes, God?" His hands were so big and strong that when you shook hands with him, you hoped he wouldn't be too friendly and enthusiastic and crush your bones. He was working at two jobs to support his large family, and there were endless stories and jokes about Don and his company, the A-1 Cesspool Company.

Sometimes at church people would ask what he did for a living, and he would reply, "I'm a sanitation engineer." I guess that was because we were surrounded by so many space engineers! When speaking about his business he would often refer to it as a "crappy business." It was never a source of embarrassment to him, but became a springboard for his great humor. Once he told one of his customers that he'd fallen into a cesspool the night before. The man was aghast! "You're kidding!" he said. "No," said Don, "I couldn't swim, but I sure went through the movements!" He would always tease me about coming to church with an alarm wrist watch. He threatened that if I went over twenty minutes with my sermon the alarm on his watch would sound.

Big Don died of a stroke about a year ago. His inner strength and his tolerance for pain were so great that his family actually believed that he could whip death with one hand tied behind him. But his stroke was so massive, that he didn't have a chance. A lot of people did not mourn, but were grateful for knowing Don DeMars.

The DeMars children received the same charisma from their parents. After the first couple of weeks when the new church had held its first services in a woman's clubhouse, I met with some of the teenagers and said I would like to start a youth group. I will never forget Patty, the oldest of the children who said "Sure, Pastor Ken. How many kids do you want?"

"Oh," I said, "as many as you can bring."

"O.K.," said Patty, "We'll just invite all our friends,

pick them up and bring them to church on Sunday evening."

Within about two weeks we had a very large youth program. They elected a Lutheran president; the vice-president was a Methodist; and the secretary-treasurer, a Roman Catholic.

Donnie DeMars is a story in himself. Of the six children who contracted polio, he was the one most afflicted physically.

He had so many talents whether in art, humor or as a scholar, it was only natural I didn't even see his handicaps until he became a boxing instructor with me when we had an athletic program in our church. He became a champion ping-pong player in a high school of 3,500 kids. He was so good at ping-pong, even with a wounded wing, that he could beat everyone but me. I was not as good as Donnie, but I would psych him out and make him feel guilty for trying to beat his minister. Now as I look back, he may have just been trying to be kind, but I guarantee you, I showed him no mercy with a ping-pong paddle.

Everywhere he would go on the campus he was like a great philosopher. Young people would gather around to listen to every word that he had to say.

Donnie and I became very close, and I think it was because of our relationship, that Donnie decided that he would enter a seminary eventually and study for the ministry.

To say that the DeMars children were winners growing up is an understatement. Their academic achievements in school were amazing. They amassed seven American Legion Awards, two Daughters of the American Revolution Awards, and countless athletic awards. Twenty student body offices were held by DeMars children.

With all this as something of an introduction I want to have Donnie tell you his own story.

Donnie's Story

It all started in the late summer of 1951. My little brother Richard became extremely feverish and my mother took him to our family doctor. The diagnosis was unsure, but he was rushed to general hospital where the diagnosis was confirmed: polio. That very night, I myself was rushed to the hospital with a temperature of 107°. Again, it was polio. Over the next three days, the nightmare became all the more unbelievable. As the hours passed, six out of eight children were stricken.

I had been in an iron lung in a coma for fourteen days with a death temperature of 108° and it didn't look as if I would make it through the night. This drama continued for many months.

An interesting comment might be made at this point. Once when I asked my dad what had held him together during this time, he answered, "Your mother." And this answer was likewise echoed by my mother, as she said, "Your father." What they had between the two of them enabled them to rise to whatever the occasion demanded.

My brother David, when he was considerably younger, had a recurring dream. He had watched the movie, *One Million, B.C.* on television, and one part where a volcano erupted, he could not get out of his mind. As the burning lava flowed down the volcano's side in the movie, it covered over a mother running with a child on her back.

But David's dream was different. As the lava flowed down the mountainside, the running woman was mother, and she had all of us children on her back. As the lava was about to cover us all, mother stopped and looked at the lava—and the lava retreated up the mountain! There could be no more pointed example of how all of us children innately felt about our parents; no matter what the catastrophe, with mother and dad we could lick the world!

My father's capacities were equally as strong as my mother's, but they were different. My mother convinced us that we had within us the capacity to do whatever we wanted. It was my father who challenged us to go after it.

If it would have been only up to my mother, we wouldn't have had to do or prove anything; we had already arrived. All she wanted was to love us and to keep us close to her.

My father loved us too, but he wanted a lot more than that. He wanted his sons to excel in what sports they could, he wanted them to bring home good grades, and he wanted us to stand on our own two feet and face the world. He insisted that his children carry for themselves the same self-integrity that he had.

In a large family you tend to divide up the responsibilities. When it was my turn to cut the grass, I told my dad that I couldn't do it. It took strong arms to push the mower, and my arms were extremely weak. My dad convinced me that I could and would do it. I got so mad at him for being so insensitive to poor little me that I went out and cut the grass. At first, it was a joke. I tried to push, but my arms kept bending, and the mower handle kept planting itself in my stomach. I got an idea. I leaned my stomach onto the handle and pushed with my whole body; it moved! That is the way I learned to cut the grass, one yard at a time.

My Own Thoughts about Myself

I am a product of my parents. Although each of the six children in our family who contracted polio were affected in different ways and in different degrees, our adjustments, recoveries and attitudes have been affected equally; it was a group happening. We all went through it, and through the understanding, the grace and the strength of our parents, we have all been made whole.

After the initial shock of the hospitalization, and the disease had run its course, I was confined to an iron lung. This eighteen month period of recuperation was the first phase of my polio experience and lasted for two years.

I do remember clearly when my limbs started returning in feeling and in movement. The disease had burned its way through my body in a diagonal way. My left upper side and lower right leg were hardest hit. My right fingers began to come back first and then my left toes. Soon I was able to bend my entire leg. I can't relate to you the joy I felt at being able to do just that. My left arm and right leg just lay there. I was encouraged to use the good limbs to help the slow ones, and after many months of physical therapy, all of them returned in fairly good measure except my left arm.

Returning home from the hospital was the most incredible day of my life. I felt in a very strange way as if I had never been gone. In all of my life, I had never felt any different than anybody else. How radically this was to change I was soon to find out.

When the time came for me to return to school, it was the recommendation of the school system that I should be placed in a school for the handicapped. My first day at Leroy Loman School for the Handicapped, was not school as I had remembered. In Watertown, South Dakota, I had excelled in almost everything. Loman School was different. There were many grades in one room and very little education. School had always been a challenge, but there was no challenge here at all.

After a few short weeks at Loman, the school's orthopedic surgeon, Dr. Albert Leviton recommended that I have a spinal operation. It was to take approximately one year for the surgery and recuperation. The muscles in the left side of my back were apparently no longer able to support me, and I had developed a scoliosis or curvature of the spine. If allowed to go unchecked, I would end up extremely deformed and twisted. My parents consented.

The following year was spent in a large turnbuckle cast.

When the recuperation was complete, I returned to Loman School and spent a short time there. I finally convinced my parents that I was ready for junior high school and because of my age, I was started in the A-7. This was to become the most challenging period in my entire life.

The very first day in junior high school was a major trauma. I was different. I limped, I had uneven shoulders, and my left arm, was decidedly smaller than my right.

There was one particular boy in junior high school that thought this was extremely funny. This boy used to call me "limpy" and "crip" and other fancy names, and received a big thrill by following in my footsteps and stepping on my heels. The result was always the same: I would trip and fall flat on my face with my books going in all directions.

On one particular day, as he started to step on my heels, I got so mad that I turned and hit him in the face with everything that I had. My dad had always told me: "If you ever have to fight a bully, hit him in the nose as hard as you can!" The boy went down! There was only one problem; he got up again! With much more power than I had hit him, he hit me back and I hit the pavement. In a matter of seconds, the entire area was filled with students, and a passing teacher took us to the principal for a good reprimand. When I walked out after seeing the principal, I was the school hero, and the other boy, who was later to become one of my best friends, was the school outcast for hitting me back.

This became one of the turning points in my own good feelings about myself. I had stood up and been strong at a point in my life where I needed to be strong. This proved I was capable of rising to the occasion, and that in so doing I found acceptance and support from those around me.

It was during this major period of adjustment that my adolescent identity search found food and growth. My family became involved with a new and energetic church that was led by a young and talented pastor named Kenneth J. Olson. He did everything right. His preaching, gymnastics, boxing, storytelling, ping-pong, and anything else you would care to name were just about everything a young guy could hope to look up to. He was my model in all things, and I tried to be like him.

There was another young man in our church named Wes Neal who was just about the best physical specimen anywhere around. One week after he announced that he was going to go into the ministry, I also decided that this would be my choice. I really believed that this was God's path for my life, and I applied myself to my books with a frenzy. The decision to enter the ministry was an important step in my life. It gave me a goal, a purpose and an identity for my life.

With increasing confidence, each day brought new challenges and new opportunities for alternate solutions. Some individuals adjust to tragedy and rehabiliate themselves. Others do not. My father always said, "No investment, no return." The future was a great deal to invest in, and the return of my life has been the prize.

How does one open a beer can when you can't hold the can in your other hand? Why, of course, you put the beer in a drawer, lean your hip against it, and with your free hand you open the beer. I found a multitude of these kinds of challenges. I learned to tie my shoes with one hand, to tie my tie with one hand, and even play ping-pong, serving and paddling with the same hand. The central fact that had been driven home to me by my mother, that I was no less the person because I had a few less tools, drove me to find creative solutions to everything.

It is in my father's gift of humor that I found a constant refuge during the frightening times. I have always loved to make people laugh. Confronting people with my handicap oftentimes created ambivalent relationships, and humor was just the remedy! Humor has a way of forcing joy into those life situations where it is having a hard time breaking in. When I ran for the student body vice-presidency in school, I told a joke about the principal at the election assembly that brought the house down, and I won the election by a landslide. I won the Senior Class Presidency in college by making a joke about the character in a man's limp; it just so happened that my competitors for the office both limped as well.

I can remember another example of how my humor seemed to rise to the occasion. I went in for my second spinal fusion at the age of twenty-six.

As they cleaned and prepared my back the day before my last stage of surgery, they took a small window of plaster out of the cast and put it on my bed. I had recently been reading Demosthenes and had written down a few of the quotes which appealed to me. As I spotted the window of the cast laying beside me, I picked up my felt pen and printed one of the quotes from Demosthenes on the cast. It went something like this: "If and when a man attempts to raise the level of life, let him do it boldly but with trembling." As I looked at the quote I thought it was a bit serious, and so I wrote underneath: FREE TRANSLATION: "Give it your best shot, guys, but don't sew up the tools inside."

The morning of my surgery, they started the anesthetic and turned me in a prone position. I will never forget how I passed into unconsciousness amidst the laughter of the doctors. They had discovered the quote on the inside of my cast.

If there is one major fear which followed me into my adult years it was my fear of confrontation with the opposite sex. I had many dates in school, but these were all very safe. The dates never went beyond the kissing stage, and I entered my first major love affair having never confronted a girl with my shirt off. I had never even been to the beach with a girl.

After college I had the opportunity to go to Europe, and I grabbed it. While I was gone I wrote to a girl from my home church, and she wrote avidly back to me. When I returned home we agreed that the whole thing was meant to be. Within three years we were married. In all of that time she had never seen me without my shirt.

One night during our early dating, I had said to her, "You know you are getting a chicken with a broken wing, don't you?" She looked at me, squeezed my hand and said, "Donnie, it doesn't matter to me." Although this eventually led me to ask her to marry me, I still in my own mind wondered if I would ever find anyone to accept me as I had myself.

The final answer came the night we were married. I was still afraid to take my shirt off in all of the glaring lights of our motel room, so I turned them all off. My wife saw right through me, but she did not turn them on. As we embraced each other in our nakedness for the first time, and she touched my back and shoulders and arms, I was finally convinced she loved me for what I was. This acceptance by her was instrumental in making me whole as a man, in control of myself and my own destiny.

Conclusions

It is interesting that when you look at the dictionary definition of cripple, you are left with a picture of someone who is less than human. He creeps or limps; he is disabled, deficient or ineffective in a specialized manner or fashion; he is something flawed or imperfect; he is deprived of strength, efficiency, wholeness or capability for service. These are all negative definitions that tend to describe or define a cripple in terms of his usefulness. That is society's problem, because it has found no adequate program to creatively use the talents of different people, or people outside of the norm.

I always hated the thought of being useless. I think this is the predominant reason why I stuck with the ministry for so very long. The ministry made me feel useful. People were dependent on me, and I liked that feeling. When I came to a gut-level realization that I was in the ministry just for myself, I left that vocation just one short year before ordination. If a minister cannot truthfully say that his greatest goal is to help people to grow up and become independent of him, then he had better choose another calling.

Although I have many deep and probing thoughts about physical stigma which are beyond the scope of these few pages, I will say a few things. Man has always lived in a competitive, aggressive and unmerciful society. We encounter each other first with curiosity, and the very last with sensitivity. We have always been caught up in a drive to have and to know but very seldom to feel.

The average and normal individual, let alone the different, has always had to fight to stay alive and retain his identity. In the need to conform to fit in, we expect everyone to be alike. The individual is an outcast.

In our cosmetic approach, we camouflage ourselves to be what society wants us to be. We have become so visually conditioned to what we expect things to be, that the different and unexpected we would rather not confront. Society still is playing games in its coming to grips with the different; the progress is slow.

As I stand and I look at my life, and I wonder what it was that enabled me to climb up out of what I came through and face life confidently and hopefully, I know in full measure what the answer is: I was loved! At the lowest and most difficult and most frightening times of my life, I was loved. That is the hope for us all. To be truly loved is to know deep within yourself that all is well.

HOW LONG DO YOU WANT TO LIVE?

There once was a very wise teacher, who always seemed to have the right answer to each problem presented to her by the members of her class. One day a boy decided to place the teacher in an impossible situation. No matter how she answered his question it could be the wrong answer. He came before the class with a small bird he had found and said, "Tell me, teacher, since you are so wise, is the bird in my hand dead or alive?" If the teacher replied "Dead," the boy would open his hand and let the little bird fly away. If the teacher answered, "The bird is alive," the boy would squeeze his hand until the bird was dead and then show the teacher a dead bird. But since the teacher was very wise, she simply replied, "Whether the bird is alive or dead, it's as you decide."

How long do you want to live? It's as you decide! For man is that unique creature who does not just repeat that pattern of his existence, but is continually asking the "why?" of his existence.

I must make it clear that when I talk of life, it is more than just existence. It's more than just how many birthdays a person had until his life was snuffed out.

The question "How long do you want to live?" is a somewhat strange question in our youth-oriented society. One where turning thirty for some is a crisis; where growing old is for someone else. Life for some is for swinging and swapping.

Then why is it I see so many unhappy swingers in therapy, who can no longer hide behind their synthetic laughter, their mod clothes, and too much alcohol? The term "beautiful people" is basically used to describe external appearances and a frenzied life-style. It's the show. It's what's up front that counts. But do we see a person's inner beauty? In fact, do we even know what to look for in other people, much less in ourselves? Do we recognize true meaning and beauty?

How many people do you admire for their zest for life? No matter how old they are, they are still full of wonder and amazement at life around them. These people seem to have found a sense of meaning and purpose to their life. I know some people like this, and to be with them is to be captured by the power of their presence. It feels good!

Albert Einstein once said, "The fairest thing we can experience is the mysterious. It is the fundamental devotion that stands at the cradle of true art and true science. He who knows it not, can no longer wonder, no longer feel amazement . . . is as good as dead, a snuffed out candle."

"Wait a minute," you say. "We live in a rotten time—the Vietnams, the Watergates, the cynicism, guilt, failure and paranoia." We should gain some perspective of history. Man's history has always had that side of it which shows his inhumanity to man.

I shall always remember the first time I read Victor Frankel's account of his experiences in a German death camp in the book *From Death Camp to Existentialism*, and his constant quote from Nietzsche, saying "He who has a 'why' to live, can bear with almost any 'how.' "

Nor shall I ever forget the night that I heard Frankel speak in person in Berkeley, California. I guarantee you that if you or I ever attempt to indulge in self-pity, the book which is now entitled *Man's Search for Meaning*[1] will turn off our negative tapes called *The Ain't Fair Blues*.

Under the most dehumanizing and deprived condition, barely existing in the shadow of a tall smokestack, Frankel writes of how people need to believe in the future and in some future goal; to discover a "why" in the midst of starvation, brutality and death. For those who saw no sense or purpose to life, there was no point carrying on and they soon died. It's hard to convince people in situations like this that there is something more to expect from life.

Frankel writes, "What was really needed was a fundamental change in our attitude toward life. We had to learn ourselves; and furthermore we had to teach the despairing men that it really did not matter what we expected from life, but rather what life expected from us. We needed to stop asking about the meaning of life, and instead to think of ourselves as those being questioned by life, daily and hourly. Our answers must consist, not in talk and meditation, but in right action and right conduct. Life ultimately means taking the responsibility to find the right answers to its problems, and to fulfill the task which it constantly sets before each individual. Thus, each of us is left to discover on our own our own beliefs and commitments that gives our lives meaning. This a person can only decide for himself."

One does not have to be a prophet to realize that something is drastically missing and lacking in too many of our lives. To quote T.S. Eliot's *Choruses from the Rock*,[2] "Where is the life we have lost in living? Where is the wisdom we have lost in knowledge? Where is the knowledge we lost in information? The cycles of heaven in twenty centuries bring us farther from God, and nearer to death."

From my own *personal* belief, we are in trouble because we have lost a spiritual relationship. Church attendance in the 50s showed a bandwagon of religion, full of activity and the building of churches. Everybody went to church. And then in the 60s, with the violence, the revolution on campuses, the turmoil, cities being burned, war in Vietnam and the drug culture, people were in a state of bewilderment and floundering. They withdrew from the church in disillusionment, and there seemed to be no answers. Many people said that God was dead. I think that the "God is Dead" movement reflected not so much on God's well-being, but on the emptiness and hollowness of men. And yet today, I sense a new beginning; a low-key one; people quietly searching for something more to their lives. People are discovering again the truth that man does not live by pizza and beer alone.

Years ago I remember watching a television show about a man who rode a commuter train to and from work each day. As he looked out the window he saw a rerun of his life—the turning points in his life; the alternatives that he faced; decisions that he had made; and how they affected the course of his life. After he reviewed his life, he concluded that if he were to live his life over, he would make only one change; he would take time to pick more daisies. What he was trying to say was instead of being so involved in climbing the ladder of success, always rushing to catch one more train, rushing through life to die, that he would stop, get out of the rut and routine of daily life and pick more daisies. He would slow down and meditate, and be refreshed by the beauty of God's world.

I don't know how many years ago I saw that program on television—maybe fifteen—but I saw myself as the one compulsively rushing through life. It's no coincidence that each spring our home in the desert in Arizona is surrounded by beautiful African daisies. I know that I need to be constantly reminded to take time to pick more daisies; to quietly greet a sunrise in the desert, and gratefully enjoy the wild quail, doves and other birds and animals that come and feed in our yard each day. I'm reminded of a friend who said a long time ago, "Don't worry about *things*. You already have life and a body, and they are far more important than what you eat or wear. Birds don't worry about what to eat. Our Heavenly Father feeds them, and you are far more valuable to him than they are. Will your worries add a single moment to your life?"[3]

If I asked you to name your most valuable possession you might be startled for a moment and begin to think of material things, or even your family, but I'm sure after a moment's reflection I could convince you that your most valuable possession is your health. You could be a millionaire, but if you were paralyzed, what value would money have without your physical and emotional health?

Now if you will agree with me that physical and emotional health is our most valuable possession, why do we say on one hand we value health and life and still do so many self-destructive things to ourselves? Since we have been warned about smoking cigarettes, we are smoking more cigarettes than ever before. We eat too much, but we are not winning our fight against being overweight. We eat too little of the foods which provide us with good nutrition. A news report said recently that 50 percent of teenagers in America suffer from malnutrition. This is not due to poverty, but to our poor dietary habits, laced with too many junk foods and sugar. We drink alcohol to the point that alcoholism is the number one drug problem of teenagers and adults. We believe too much in magic pills from the medicine man to take away all of our worries for the day. We exercise too little, and wonder why we are sluggish and prone to heart attacks. We are more concerned about the maintenance of our automobiles than we are about our physical and emotional health.

Health and Medical Services

Critical problems in the health professions—the high cost of medical and hospital service, insurance problems, financial liability, malpractice, poor distribution of physicians—are highly vital issues today. They are so vital, that I must admit they are beyond the scope of this book, and the solutions beyond my expertise.

The basic issue I would like to discuss is that of health

or disease as a philosophy for the healing professions.

The philosophy of a health model versus a disease model in treating people is at the core of so many of the problems I have listed previously. Health insurance companies reward people for being sick and hospitalized. It does not pay, generally, for office visits designed to keep a person healthy and out of the hospital. Even if the physician hospitalizes a person, and has done a recent series of tests, these most likely will be repeated in the hospital along with a great many more than may be necessary, because this is a source of income to the hospital. With the problems of malpractice, physicians are practicing defensive medicine and ordering more tests than necessary as a hedge against a lawsuit.

When a person becomes sick, it's a great temptation to get a lot of mileage out of being sick and being the center of attention. How many times we make jokes about "Let me tell you about my operation," or "If you think you have it bad, just let me tell you about my miserable health!"

I remember the time that the minister in our church in Phoenix, Pete Lindsay, took his 5-year-old Linda with him on a sick call one Sunday afternoon at a nursing home. When Pastor Pete asked a woman, "How's everything going?" she told him, and told him, and told him for an hour about how miserable she was. Finally he broke into the recitation and said, "Let's pray." After a short prayer he turned and walked out with his daughter who turned at the doorway and said to the lady, with a child's truth, "You take an enema, and you'll feel a lot better."

We have VA hospitals and disability insurance which

serve a meaningful purpose, but there is also a subtle tendency to reward a person for being ill, and to make it too profitable for him financially to admit that he is well and able to function. If a person gives up these advantages and takes the responsibility for his own support, then it would cost him financial benefits.

One of the most difficult challenges I meet in therapy, are not in the nature of the problems a person has, but in the training and encouragement a person receives from physicians and families on how to be a miserable patient. By becoming a patient, the person is relieved of the personal responsibility for his health as well as personal responsibility for getting better. Self-pity is the most destructive of all narcotics.

Jesus once came upon a man who had been ill for thirty-eight years. He had been lying by the pool of Bethesda, waiting to be healed. When the water was stirred up by an angel the first person into the water was the only one healed. In all those years he had never made it in time. Jesus said to him, "Do you want to be healed?" The fact he had been there a long time gave evidence of a desire to be healed, but he had been waiting for somone to help him into the pool. Now he was faced with a piercing, personal responsibility for his own health, and was told to rise, take up his pallet and walk. He took responsibility for his health, he obeyed and was healed.[4]

The power of healing is in each of us. Physicians only prepare the way and the process for healing to occur. A physician can do everything in his power to save a life, but if a person says no to life, he becomes worse and eventually dies.

No one can be responsible ultimately for the ques-

tion; "How long do you want to live?" but you . . . .
it's as you decide!

Since 1965, I have developed an ever-increasing interest and dedication to the dental profession. People are always perplexed when they see the certificate in my office that I belong to the American Society for Preventive Dentistry or when they know that I am leaving town for a speaking engagement in dentistry.

Truthfully, I was invited to a study club of Dentists in Phoenix in 1965 to talk about the art of listening and communication as it would apply to dentistry. Later I became very dedicated to dentistry when I was asked to be a teacher on a dental seminar for husbands and wives in Maui, Hawaii. I became so dedicated to dentistry that I rededicate myself at least once or twice a year by going to Maui!

Seriously, dentistry has been built on a disease model, rather than on a health model. The results of dental care have not been satisfactory, either to the patient or the dentist.

An article in the *National Observer*,[5] reported that, according to the United States Public Health Service, 98 percent of all Americans have cavities. The average American has five unfilled cavities, and half of all children have at least one by the age of two years. Twenty million of 110 million adults have lost all of their teeth. Another 22.5 million suffer from severe periodontal problems. Half the nation's children have gingivitis (an inflamation of the soft gum tissue that often leads to periodontal disease).

Dental disease is a major health problem, affecting

everyone in the United States. And yet it is probably one of the most ignored health problems we have. People take better care of their armpits than they do their mouths. And yet from an interpersonal point of view, we never kiss armpits, but we kiss mouth-to-mouth. Seldom does anyone ever die from complications arising from dental disease.

It's tragic that people will so passively and apathetically accept slow destruction of their mouth when dental disease could be as rare as polio. The mouth is a primary sex contact between people. It is the very emotional center of a person's being. Yet why are so many people willing to commit oral suicide?

It starts with the training of a dentist. Dental education is changing rapidly, but most dentists spend their first year in dental school making false teeth, and some never get over it. Isn't it a positive reinforcement about the inevitability of dental disease—that people will leave the world the way they enter—gumming it?

Dentists aren't alone in the initial impact of their schooling. First year medical students start working with a cadaver and many of *them* never get over it. Cadavers never talk back, so neither should patients. It is the beginning of depersonalized medicine.

Dentists are trained to work with tools, machines, materials and things called teeth. Neglected in their training is the basic fact that teeth are connected to people's emotions about fear, love, hate, guilt, youth and aging. The dental professionals, including dental hygienists, are led to the erroneous belief that they are the ones responsible for dental health of the patients. In fact they earn a living from patient's dental disease, for cleaning, polishing, filling, drilling, capping, making bridges and dentures.

Is there any hope for preventing dental disease? You and I have been told to brush our teeth twice a day, and see our dentist at least twice a year. Does that stop dental disease? No, the disease goes on. Dr. Robert Barkley has called tooth brushing the great American hoax. Dr. Barkley says that by using the brush in a highly skilled manner, you can achieve removal of bacteria from about 85 percent of your tooth surface. This is where about 15 percent of your dental disease originates.

The 15 percent that you consistently miss is where 85 percent of all dental disease occurs. In other words, there is a fungus among us—in our mouth—that's causing dental disease. As Roger Miller wrote in his song, *You Can't Roller Skate in a Buffalo Herd*, you can't get a tooth brush between your teeth to remove and disorganize a colony of bacteria called plaque. The problem is not that we have bacteria, in our mouth, but the state of disorganization of the bacteria colonies is the factor. Flossing between the teeth and around the gum lines with toothbrushing disorganizes the colonies of bacteria which take about 30 hours to reorganize. Just remember, 30 hours after you've gone for your six-month examination and had your teeth cleaned, the plaque is back at work unless it's thoroughly disorganized every 24-hours, and not promoted by being fed refined sugar.

A large percentage of dentists recognize the need to change and improve their skills in working with people. Modern high-speed drills, analgesics for reducing pain, dental assistants to speed up the time, and many more new skills and interest in preventing dental disease and teaching people good nutrition are happening, but dentists need your assistance to help the profession change from a disease profession to a health profession.

First you must make a decision to be the one responsible for the health of your oral cavity. If you want a disease contract with your dentist say, "Look, doctor, I fully realize that with a disease contact I am in charge of the relationship as a dental patient. All I expect from you is to slow down the disease process, fill teeth, relieve me from pain from an abcessed tooth, pull teeth that can't be saved, fix up the destructive aftermath from dental disease with crowns and bridges—and then eventually fit me with dentures."

Remember the dental disease contract is very expensive. It costs thousands of dollars, hours of time waiting in dental offices, sitting in a dental chair, walking the floor at night with a throbbing toothache and finally receiving substitute teeth as the grand prize.

I'm serious when I say you have a right to choose dental *disease* contracts as a basis for your relationship to the dental profession. You also have the right to a dental *health* relationship with the dental profession. A dental health contract means that you assume primary personal responsibility for maintaining a healthy oral cavity, with a dental team as a supporting cast. The goal of a dental health contract is to save your teeth, money, time, pain and let you have a youthful mouth as long as you live. Remember dental health isn't expensive, but dental disease is very expensive. If you want to see a shocked dentist and a perplexed dental staff, just talk to them about the following subjects before any treatment is initiated unless it is a painful toothache:

1. Start off by stating that you want a health contract and that you realize that the responsibility for maintaining the health of the oral cavity is in your hands.

2. Ask the dentist and his staff to teach you to have a healthy mouth; to teach you how to floss daily to disorganize the colonies of bacterial plaque; to analyze your nutritional habits and recommend a good nutritional life style. If they haven't fainted by then, you can ask them if they are engaged in preventive dentistry. Ask for a thorough exam. Be sure to ask the dentist and his staff about health problems you would like to discuss, allergies to medications, any stresses and changes in your life in the past year and how they may have affected the health of the tissue in your mouth. Ask for a complete set of x-rays. Since dentists are not all equal in ability, be wary of a dentist who is eager to pull your teeth and sell you dentures. A good exam will include a screening for cancer and a discussion about the health of the gum tissue.

Bleeding gums are a sign of a periodontal disease. Periodontal disease is very sneaky and often painless, but is so destructive that if it is not corrected it can result even in bone loss. Your dentist may take a routine blood pressure.

If you are having a headache that starts where the jawbone is connected to your ear, you may have a faulty occlusion which is the way the teeth fit, or don't fit, as they come together. If you are grinding your teeth at night, talk to a dentist about it. There should be an open and free discussion of fees for service. Don't fuss about a fee for learning how to prevent dental disease. It is the best money you will ever spend for dental health insurance.

A health contract will help you keep your teeth, save you money and pain for the rest of your life. That's something worth smiling about, isn't it?

Now you've heard my dentistry spiel . . . thank you! But it does stress the need for a shift from disease model to health model.

As a psycho-therapist, I focus upon what's eating a person, and how his negative tapes can be very destructive to his emotional life as well as his physical being. I try to take a multifaceted approach to understand a person. What a person thinks and experiences emotionally can effect his digestive process; alter his delicate endocrine balance; cause changes in blood pressure; cause changes in the temperature of the body; cause the skin to erupt with disorders. Over a long period of emotional stress, physiological changes can occur which cause a person to become susceptible to a disease.

When I began to read and hear more and more about nutrition and health, I first reacted indifferently and apathetically. Fanatics have always pushed my "off" button. The medical profession was quick to dispute and debunk articles and books on vitamins, diets and other claims made by nutrition people.

Then I began to realize that the average physician knows little or nothing about nutrition because it was a very neglected field of study in medical school. When a person thinks he has all the answers, any new data to the contrary can easily be dismissed by a wave of the hand. I tried to learn what I could about nutrition and its aid to health. I am a long way from being an expert, but I do feel that more good scientific research is needed.

Let's see where we can share some common experiences. Have you ever tried a fad or crash diet to lose weight? How did you feel when you were dieting? Did you become nervous, jittery, depressed or short tempered? Did you suffer anxiety and poor sleep? Furthermore, did you ever take diet pills or diet shots to help you lose weight fast, and then feel like you were wired with nervous energy or at times like you were losing your mind? After all this self-induced torture, did you keep the weight off or gain it all back? When a person has suffered so much on a diet, he deserves to reward himself and reverts to the old eating pattern that made him overweight in the beginning. So he yo-yos through life!

The medical profession has come to the conclusion that diet pills and shots are not useful and should not be used for losing weight. They can be dangerous to emotional stability as well as play havoc with metabolic balance. The answer to being overweight is a complete change of life-style so that one receives the optimum nutritional value in food with the proper vitamins and minerals.

The first step is to eliminate refined sugars. Sugar is dangerous? Are you kidding?

No! I'm not kidding. Dr. John Yudkin makes these two bold statements in his book *Sweet and Dangerous*:[6] (1) There is no physiological requirement for sugar. All human nutritional needs can be met in full without having to take a single spoon of white, raw or brown sugar. (2) If only a small fraction of what is known about the effects of sugar were to be revealed in relation to other material used as a food additive, the material would promptly be banned. Sugar consumption has risen close to an annual 120 pounds per person. In terms of the sugar intake on a weekly basis, the average person eats nothing but sugar every fourth day.

In an article by Clair Pierre, entitled *The Nutrition Dilemma*,[7] it is estimated that the U.S. pays a health bill of 30 billion dollars annually for illnesses related to faulty nutrition. Junk food, candy, snack foods—donuts, potato chips, soft drinks, etc.—account for more than 35 percent of a typical American family's food budget.

Research is linking the rise of hyperactivity in children to food additives like food coloring. Cholesterol-rich diets, with hydrogenated fats, disturb the cholesterol metabolism. This does not help prevent heart disease.

Nutritional deficiencies are not confined to the poor, but are rampant among the privileged and affluent, and especially the young people in our country. The result, says Pierre, is an unbelievable roster of diet-linked diseases. Diabetes, hypertension and obesity and its potential dysfunctions of kidney, liver and gall bladder. Anemia is widespread among adolescent girls. Dental decay, hypoglycemia, even retardation and arthritis are on the suspected list, and so are certain kinds of mental illness (these are a matter of great controversy).

The brain cells are fed by the blood and what it brings in it. Some exciting research shows evidence that some forms of depression may be induced by a lack of essential amino acids from protein to nourish the brain cells.

For years medicine has known that alcoholics frequently suffer from malnutrition but the malnutrition was thought to be the result of the alcoholism and not a participating factor predisposing or causing alcoholism. Dr. Roger Williams in his book, *Nutrition Against Disease*[8] strongly states that no one who follows good nutrition practices ever becomes alcoholic. Dr. Williams conducted research to show that the wrong diet can create an alcoholic.

One group of rats on high-carbohydrate diet drank the equivalent of a human's consumption of a quart of 100 proof whiskey a day. The second group of rats were on a high-carbohydrate diet fortified with vitamins and minerals. They consumed only 1/3 as much alcohol as the first group. The third group, on a nutritionally balanced human diet, generally preferred water instead of alcohol. In group one, after several weeks, sugar was added to the alcohol solution and these rats became even heavier drinkers. When they were put on a balanced diet, they gradually became ex-alcoholics. Dr. Williams' research has been duplicated at Loma Linda University in California.

One of the first questions I ask an ex-alcoholic now is to tell me what and when he eats during an average day. Very often the ex-alcoholic follows the same poor nutritional eating pattern he had before and during his alcoholism. I wonder if this is why there are so many dry alcoholics who are difficult to live with. Their spouses sometimes secretly wish that their partner would go back to drinking alcohol because they were *almost* easier to live with!

Dr. Cheraskin and Dr. Ringsdorf talk about the optimal diet in their book *Psycho-Dietetics*,[9] in which good nutrition includes meat, seafood and poultry. Foods should not be fried. Fresh vegetables and fruits are necessary. Whole grain foods with no chemical additives, dry roasted nuts, unhydrogenated peanut butter are fine. Foods to be used sparingly are butter on potatoes and vegetable oil. One should reduce the intake of salt, coffee and tea. Avoid such foods as sugar, hydrogenated fat, food preservatives such as nitrates and nitrites, artificial flavoring and coloring additives.

These comments on nutrition are to open your thinking processes and to encourage you to explore this exciting field. I don't believe anyone has all the answers, but it is worthwhile trying to understand the whole person and to explore the whole field of nutrition. Good nutrition is one of the ways to good health, and to keeping your health.

Emotional Health

Many men do not know how to express their emotions, such as anger and joy, love and sorrow. So their bodies convert these repressed emotions into coronaries, headaches and depressions. The art of play is fun as a participant—but its easily forgotten in the business of earning a living and raising a family. Then we wait to be entertained by television. People sometimes are so programmed that the only way they can allow themselves to play is to make work out of their play.

But there is a change, a new sign of hope. Quietly and without great to-do, thousands of people are jogging in the morning and being more concerned about their health. We see groups like Weight Watchers and they are having success. Alcoholics Anonymous is reaching thousands of people that traditional psychotherapists have not been able to reach before. We are beginning to learn and believe in change and to value again our precious gift called health.

I have learned that I can't afford the expensive destructiveness of bitterness and hate that could consume me. I can't let yesterday's insults and hurts grow and destroy me today.

> *I've shut the door on yesterday and its sorrows*
> *   and mistakes.*
> *I've locked within its gloomy walls past failures*
> *   and heartaches;*
> *And now I've thrown the key away to seek another*
> *   room;*
> *I'll furnish it with hope and smiles and every*
> *   springtime bloom.*
> *No thought shall enter this abode that has a*
> *   hint of pain*
> *And every malice and distrust shall never*
> *   therein reign.*
> *I've shut the door on yesterday and thrown the*
> *   key away.*
> *Tomorrow holds no doubt for me since I have*
> *   found today.*
>
> Anonymous

True, we live in a stress-filled world, but one of the

most difficult problems to be resolved is that of how to use unstructured time.

John Paul Sartre's play on Hell, called *No Exit,* is all about a room full of people who are there forever. Finally someone says at the end of the play, "Hell is other people."

To break out of the boredom man needs to find meaning to his life. For men whose life has been so identified with their work, when they retire, so does their life. Tragically, retirement for them is a void of boredom because they hadn't developed any other facets to their personality. They are merely killing time while awaiting death.

Marriage can become a routine and a monotonous sameness, as can many jobs which serve as a means to earning a livelihood. The sadness of boredom is that a person has never believed that he is a potent source of power, talent and resources.

Life for me is so exciting and I have so much curiosity to be satisfied, that even when I die, look out! I may just jump out of my coffin and say, "Wait a minute! There is one more thing I would like to try."

Believe me, if you want to grow and never be bored, be prepared to be open to new ideas. Remember the purpose is growth, not perfection.

The Stress of Your Life

In 1965, one of the most intriguing and though-provoking books I read was entitled *The Stress of Life*[10] by Hans Selye. Selye's dedication was enough to hook my curiosity because it's dedicated to those who are not afraid to enjoy the stress of a full life, nor too naïve to think that they can do so without intellectual effort.

One nice thing about the word "stress" is that it is so easily understood compared to so many of the medical terms. Selye is quick to point out that stress is a part of life. To live without stress is a condition described as "rigor followed by mortis." Stress, basically, is the rate of wear and tear on the body. In Selye's words "Stress is the non-specific response the body makes to any demands made upon it."

Stress is not always bad, but can be the stimulus to growth and challenge to the human body. The secret is for each person to discover his limits and ability to cope with stress with his body and his life style. When stress becomes distress, then there are three stages the organism experiences in coping with distress syndrome, which is called the general adaptation syndrome. The three stages are: (1) the alarm reaction; (2) the stage of resistance when defensive mechanisms of the organism are activated; (3) the stage of exhaustion.

Selye states that when the brain signals the attack of a stressor, the pituitary and adrenal glands produce such harmones as ACTH, cortisone and cortisole, which activate protective bodily reactions.

Have you ever been angry, frightened, preparing to fight or just receive some bad news and you experience a sudden surge of energy or stimulation of adrenalin? This is a state of alarm or first response to stress, which activates a chemical output to the body defenses.

On an international scale for example, the country of Israel surprised the world with its six-day war and victory over the Arab nations. The victory did not bring peace, but continued preparation for another outbreak of hostilities which erupted when Egypt engaged in a surprise attack on Israeli forces at the Suez Canal. The war was short but costly in men and equipment on both sides. Emotionally, there were reports of some of the Israeli forces behaving very erratically, immobilized by depression. This breakdown had nothing to do with patriotism, but demonstrated the fact that no one can exist constantly in a state of alarm. In time the adaptive mechanisms to fight stress are depleted. The person is overwhelmed and enters a state of exhaustion and depression.

Each person is unique—genetically and metabolically —and has his own unique neural rate of activity. He is unique in the way he experiences life and the decisions he makes about what is going to determine his emotional well-being.

One of the points to which Selye calls attention—quite a frightening one—is that "each person's supply of adaptive energy is like our nation's ore deposits. Once it's burned up, it's gone! And so is a person! We don't die of old age, but some organ or disease process has caused a breakdown in our body."

As a psychologist, I am very aware of how negative tapes can have a destructive affect upon them physically. I am sure you have known people who have experimented traumatic shocks and after you haven't seen them for a while, are shocked at how much they have aged by being overwhelmed by stress. The adaptive energy is depleted and aging is the result.

When stress has overwhelmed a person he becomes a ready recipient for a disease process. A famous Canadian clinician, Sir William Ostler, said, "It is much more important to know what sort of a patient has a disease, than what sort of disease a patient has."

Claude Bernard, a renowned 19th century French physiologist, believed that disease is resisted by a central equilibrium within the patient. Bernard said, "Illnesses hover constantly about us—they are seeds blown by the wind, but they do not take root in the terrain unless it is ready to receive them." By the terrain, Bernard meant the body, a collection of cells and systems constantly shifting, altering and adjusting to the pressures from within and without.

Although Louis Pasteur disagreed with Claude Bernard during his lifetime, Pasteur's dying words were these: "Bernard was right. The microbe is nothing, the terrain is everything."

During a person's life he is constantly being confronted with change, coping and stress. How a person deals with these stresses and changes is very important. You would be amazed at how often I hear people try to communicate why they are depressed and anxious, but are unaware of the impact of the cumulative power of stress and change which has assaulted their lives. It's only when I begin to ask them about a death in the family or other traumatic events that the light dawns, and they remember what has happened.

One of the problems of stress in a family is that too often each member withdraws into himself and so no one gathers strength from another.

Dr. Thomas Holmes and Dr. Richard Rahe, psychiatrists at the University of Washington, has devised a scale and assigns point values to changes that often affect us. The scale dramatically focuses on the problem of how much change a person can take within one year of his life. When the point values, for the various changes occurring in one year add up to 300 points, a person is at a critical point. With the people he has studied, 80 percent of the people who exceeded 300 points, became seriously depressed, had heart attacks, and suffered from other serious illnesses.

LIFE CHANGE	POINTS
Death of spouse	100
Divorce	73
Marital separation	65
Jail term	63
Death of close family member	63
Personal injury or illness	53
Marriage	50
Fired from job	47
Marital reconciliation	45
Retirement	45
Change in health of family member	44
Pregnancy	40
Sex difficulties	39
Gain of new family member	39
Change in financial status	38
Death of close friend	37
Change to different kind of work	36
Change in number of arguments with spouse	35
Foreclosure of mortgage or loan	30
Change in work responsibilities	29

Son or daughter leaving
home 29
Trouble with in-laws 29
Outstanding personal
achievement 28
Wife beginning or stopping
work 26
Beginning or ending school 26
Revision of personal habits 24
Trouble with boss 23
Change in residence 20
Change in schools 20
Vacation 13
Minor violations of law 11

Your Killing Personality

How long do you want to live? Your personality and
life style often answer the question for you. Drs. Meyer
Friedman and Ray Rosenman have written a book
entitled *Type A Behavior and Your Heart*[11] which reports
on the relationship between personality and heart attack.

No people cope with stress in the same way. But one
type of personality ends up with heart disease, and the
other one doesn't. In 1957 the two doctors began to
suspect that it was not just diet, smoking or lack of exercise that accounted for the rapid increase in coronary
disease in this country. They felt that the accelerated
pace at which we live had introduced a new kind of stress
and began to investigate the relationship between a person's personality and behavior pattern and susceptibility
to heart attack. Thus they emerged with Type A and Type
B personalities.

Type A personality, whether male or female, is characterized by intense drive, aggressiveness, ambition, competitiveness, pressure for getting things done and impatience, while waiting for traffic to speed up or getting a table in a restaurant.

Type A has a habit of fighting time. He feels like he is always living under a deadline. Speaks at a staccato-type rate, has a tendency to end his sentences in a rush and often interrupts others before they finished a sentence. He frequently sighs faintly between words which is a clue of exhaustion from stress. Type A doesn't have time to get sick, to get a physical or relax on a vacation, and if he plays a game it's usually a competitive game played with a grim determination to win. He is preoccupied with his work. He rushes through life and never slows down long enough to enjoy a nice meal and a glass of wine.

The acceptance of the stress and strain concept is understandable. It nourishes the ego of the believer and it is readily received by the unfortunate victim and his relatives. It makes coronary and heart disease an unjust reward for virtue. How much nicer it is when stricken with a coronary thrombosis to be told it was all due to hard work, laudable ambition and selfless devotion to duty, rather than due to gluttony and physical indolence!

Type A is driven in his work to succeed and has a tremendous need for approval by others for his success. But in his competition for the top jobs with his company, Type A often loses out to Type B because he is too competitive, too compulsive, and makes decisions too fast, in minutes, instead of waiting for more information. Type A is a number freak—life by numbers! When describing his vacation, instead of reporting on how good it felt to relax, he will tell you how many miles he drove each day and how many places he visited in two weeks. You become exhausted just listening to him.

This type of person is not creative, but give him a quota and he will go bananas trying to be the Number 1 salesman. He is a good salesman, but he makes a poor manager of people, much less a president of a corporation. The Type A man is two to three times more likely to get heart disease.

Women also have Type A personalities and as they have more opportunities to compete with men, there will be an increase in women who are equally driven in striving for achievement and climbing the ladder of success who develop a coronary profile of Type A man.

In contrast, a Type B personality is able to hang loose emotionally. He is able to work and be able to let go of his work. He is not always looking at his watch. Life is not by numbers. He is more interested in the quality of life. He does not always have to be first. He is also able to delegate responsibility, and he enjoys time out to think and be creative. Type B can enjoy many aspects of life that are not work-oriented.

Can Type A personality change? Yes, as long as we live we can learn new behavior.

If one could ask a Type A personality to describe his parents and their philosophy of raising children, he would most likely respond that they were authoritarian, achievement-oriented and gave conditional love. A child raised with criticism and fear finds it difficult to accept himself as he is, and to love himself. It is more natural for this person to feel the need to win at all costs—until one day he can receive the approval he longs for.

A Type A person who wants to change, who believes in change and is prepared to learn new behavior can be on the road to a new life, but it won't be easy.

Personal responsibility for changing is necessary, because no one can save him from a coronary, but himself. To believe in change is an act of faith for many. His drive and compulsiveness have been so much a part of him that it's only an act of faith and belief in change that can help him. But remember, we can learn new behavior.

If you are an A personality, block out on your daily schedule a list of guidelines for a new way of life, and decide to do a few of the following:

> If you start your day in such a hurry that you either rush through breakfast, or don't take time for breakfast, make a decision to get up ½ hour earlier. Start your day leisurely with breakfast. Listen to your thoughts, your tapes. If you find a negative tape filled with demanding words of "ought," and "should" and "would", turn the tape, flush it and hang loose. If this behavior seems unreal to you, it's only because it's new. Don't be discouraged. If that's how you feel, that's good, because the change may cause you to experience a sense of floundering, and it will demand that you take time to think before you act and react, in your own habitual manner.

> When you start to drive to work, stop and check your muscles. Are they tense and gripping the steering wheel? Are you driving like you are in the Indianapolis 500? If so, relax

your muscles, take a deep breath, listen to some music and say, "Car, take me to work carefully."

While at work take a 15 or 30 minute break just to listen to see if you have any negative, demanding tapes running. Plan to take a lunch hour, but don't make it one more hour of work. Instead learn how to "pick more daisies."

After lunch take a short walk, or do something to give variety to your day.

In ending your day at work, begin to use the last fifteen minutes to think, to reflect and to relax. Then go home, not tense and uptight, but emotionally mellow. This does not mean stopping on the way home and getting bombed with alcohol. Find time for quietness and think of those things you have always wanted to do and have never taken the time. Begin to say *why not?* and *please*. Talk to your marriage parner after dinner about those things you have been holding inside too long.

Learn how to play as if your life didn't depend upon it. In a way it does depend upon it.

Practice deep muscle relaxation. Tense each set of muscles for a count of five; then relax, tense and relax. Do this all over your body, visualizing your tense muscle fiber becoming as limp as a rubber band. Give yourself an hour, if possible, for this deep muscle relaxation.

Now this is heavy! Write down your own obituary. What will you say of your life? What kind of legacy will you leave your spouse and your children?

I would like to quote a famous philosopher by the name of Satchel Paige. He gives you these rules on how to keep in shape:

1. Avoid fried meats which anger up the blood.
2. If your stomach disputes you, lie down and pacify it with cool thoughts.
3. Keep the juices flowing by jangling around gently as you move.
4. Go very light on the vices such as carrying on in society. The social ramble ain't restful.
5. Avoid running at all times.
6. Don't look back, something may be gaining on you.

LET'S TALK ABOUT DEATH AND AGING

For too long people have avoided talking about death until the funeral comes along. Even now people have a way of denying the reality of death. We speak of the person who has died as not "dead," but "sleeping." The deceased is fixed up cosmetically so that everyone talks about how natural and lifelike the person appears. The bereaved family is given medication to help numb the shock of the death. Those who have lost a loved one are praised for being brave, for taking it so well and not breaking down. This can only create problems when they face delayed grief problems.

Parents have failed to talk openly and simply with their children about death. They don't explain that death is a fact of life.

I am very encouraged by the number of articles, seminars and television shows that have recently been made available to the public on the subject of Thanatology— a study of death. There have been articles written about a person's right to die; discussions on the medical and legal aspects of death by abortion, mercy killing, and euthanasia. These subjects are being brought out into the open for public exploration and discussion at last.

The minute we are born we begin to die. We will eventually be confronted with our own personal death. I wish we could all make peace with death at twenty-five so we don't have to spend the rest of our life running from it, or wasting time worrying about it. To personally accept the reality of one's own death is an awesome encounter.

When I was serving as pastor, at Grace Lutheran Church in Richmond, California, one of my first adjustments was that of coming to a church of mostly elderly people from a church made up of predominantly young people with lots of babies. I spent many afternoons visiting and having private communion with those in county hospitals and nursing homes for the elderly and chronically ill. There was also a large funeral home across the street from our chruch which was owned by a member of the church. I spent a great deal of my time, as an extension of nursing homes, and the mortuary.

If you have never visited and smelled a nursing home on a regular basis, you are fortunate. I found it very depressing and dehumanizing. How do you answer a person who says, "I have prayed to die, so why do I linger? Even if I was able to leave, why would I go home? I have nothing to live for, so why can't I die?"

Slowly, but surely, all of this began to have an effect upon me; people who waited and wanted to die, who had once led full lives. In a strange existential way, I was confronted with my own death. Facing the reality of my own death had a tremendous impact upon me, personally. I made the agonizing realization that what I feared and dreaded most wasn't so much death, but the process of dying. I was horrified at the thought of seeing myself in some smelly nursing home, over-medicated so I wouldn't make too many demands. Thus, with a chemically controlled mind and hardening arteries, I would passively await the arrival of my death.

At this time I was thirty-five-years-old, overweight and out of shape physically. I had just been told by a physician that I had begun to develop high blood pressure and, unless I changed my way of life, would be a likely candidate for a coronary within ten years.

I took a personal inventory of my life, and reflected on how I wanted to spend the rest of my years. I realized that for some time I had a deep desire to go to graduate school and become a clinical psychologist. This was in conflict with staying in the parish ministry which I also enjoyed.

I talked it over with Jeannie, and she said whatever I wanted to do would be fine with her, if it would make me happy. I wrote away to several schools and was accepted at Arizona State University. For the second time in our marriage, Jeannie had to put up with my going to graduate school, only by this time we had three children. She deserves a medal because she never complained.

Facing the inevitability of my death was a depressing encounter, but out of it came a new appreciation and wonder and thanksgiving of life. T.S. Eliot wrote these powerful words: "Though you forget the way to the Temple, there is one who remembers the way to your door. Life you may evade, but death you shall not. You shall not deny the Stranger."[1]

Men seem to have a more difficult time coming to terms

with death than women. Maybe it's the myth that men are stronger that blocks us from thinking about death until the day it hits us—"I'm getting old!"

A heart attack has a way of getting a man's attention! Too often I have seen his whole personality change. Even though he recovers from the heart attack and is able to go back to work, he suffers from a deep melancholy and is irritable and hard to live with. Instead of talking about his deepest fears and feelings with his wife or counselor, he withdraws and actually waits for the next attack.

He may, on the other hand, go to the other extreme and behave as if he had never had a heart attack and try to prove how healthy and vital he is by becoming overactive physically.

For over 20 years, one of our family's favorite friends has been Henry Calvin. I am sure he is one of your friends also, for one of the roles he played in movies and television was Sergeant Garcia in *Zorro* and brought laughter to millions. He weighed between 300 and 380 pounds. He starred in *Babes In Toyland* for Walt Disney. Even then he was asked to gain weight, to the horror of his physician. He was the strong man in *Toby Tyler and the Circus*.

One of Henry's great idols was Oliver Hardy, and after dinner he would keep you laughing for hours as he became Ollie. He was great on Dick van Dyke's show honoring Laurel and Hardy.

I don't know if many people realize Henry Calvin's great range of talent included operetta. In 1940 Henry became the bass-baritone soloist at Radio City Music Hall in New York City. He also starred in many Broadway musicals such as *The Chocolate Soldier* and *Kismet*.

Henry showed wonderful kindness to our family with free passes to Disneyland and always made our children feel very special. You couldn't help but love that big, big man. It was a painful shock for us to receive a Christmas letter in 1974 which said, "First of all it seems that I contracted 'a slight case of cancer of the throat'—you know, like being slightly pregnant—and have been in and out of hospitals all the blessed year. After all, CA is very fashionable right now." He then went on to describe the numerous surgeries and hospitalizations and how he had lost his voice box. Then he closed his letter with this sentence. "Guess what? We are having the most wonderful Christmas imaginable, because we are alive and together, and we all wish contentment and happiness for you all throughout this season and the years to come." In another letter he wrote about how it really is to enter "the world of silence." "It's not really too bad, you see. You never have to talk to anyone you don't want to. You just nod or shake your head and the meaning is perfectly clear. However, for special people like you, I can use my electronic speech device. Besides that, if you still can't understand me I can write on my 39¢ magic slate, like any other youngster learning to talk."

Though he loved to eat, he was always talking about going on a diet. He said once, "I have discovered the perfect diet. You can eat everything you want, but just don't swallow." Now, tragically, he had lost the use of his tongue and couldn't swallow, and was down to a lean 180 pounds.

I cannot but be overwhelmed by Henry's attitude, looking death in the eye, and still having a sense of humor.

I also hurt for him because I knew how he loved to sing, laugh, clown and perform.

His tremendous battle to keep the right attitude, when all the world around him was collapsing, wasn't an easy task.

Death Is an Advisor

In the book *Journey to Ixtlan*[2] by Carlos Castaneda, there is a chapter entitled, "Death Is an Advisor," which says, " 'Death is our eternal companion,' Don Juan said— with a most serious air. 'It is always to our left, at an arm's length. It was watching you when you were watching the White Falcon. It whispered in your ear and you felt its chill, as you felt it today. It has always been there watching for you. It always will, until the day it taps you.' "

Death is an advisor—if you listen to it and decide how you will live each day!

I take my family with me to seminars for work and play and we spend time together after the seminar for swimming, surfing and snorkeling and fishing. Most important I have told them that although I may not be able to leave them any money when I'm gone, I have wanted to leave them a legacy of beautiful memories. As a family we all agree that life is for building beautiful memories at each opportunity we can. For me death has been a good advisor.

A New Definition of Death and the Right to Die

When is a person dead? Webster's Dictionary defines death as a permanent cessation of all vital functions; the end of life. This was a good operational definition of death until modern medical technology reached such an advanced stage that machines could keep people alive for months and even some as long as ten years. There are accounts of people who had severe brain damage and were hooked up to machines. They were kept alive with IV's and tubes feeding them through the stomach for years, which drained away a small fortune. When they finally died, an autopsy revealed that the brain was liquified.

Now the question as to when a person is dead takes on a new definition. Is it morally right to keep someone's physical functions operative when the brain has been so damaged that he can never return to consciousness or perform anything useful, but must spend his days as a vegetable with no mind? What right does the medical profession have to bankrupt a family by running up an astronomical medical bill? Is the hospital fulfilling its function by allowing bed space to be occupied for so long, and hospital personnel to be involved with the care of such a person? Now comes an even more difficult question. Who has the authority to turn off the machines?

Out of this dilemma is coming a new definition of death called "brain death." A person is dead when he has two successive flat brain wave tests. The brain can be, for all matter and purposes, dead, but to modern technology a person can be kept alive with a dead brain. This concern is reflected in the increased number of people who are writing out and signing a Living Will. The Living Will is a legally non-binding document, which is addressed to a person's physician and family. It reads like this:

"To my family, my physicians, clergyman, my lawyer:

If the time comes when I can no longer actively take part in decisions for my own future, I wish this statement to stand as a testament of my wishes. If there is no reasonable expectations for my recovery from physical or mental and spiritual disability, I request that I be allowed to die, and not be kept alive by artificial means or heroic measures. I ask also that drugs be mercifully administered to me for terminal suffering, even if in relieving pain they may hasten the moment of death. I value life and the dignity of life, so that I am not asking that my life be directly taken, but that my dying not be unreasonably prolonged, nor the dignity of life be destroyed. This request is made after careful reflection while I am in good health and spirits. Although this document is not legally binding, you who care for me will, I hope, feel morally bound to take it into account. I recognize that this places a heavy burden of responsibility upon you, and it is with the intention of sharing this responsibility, that this statement is made."

Kenneth J. Olson
April 25, 1975

So this is one way of making public my Living Will. What I am hoping for is a good and peaceful death, with no last minute medical heroics and that my family may not face the burden of making this decision for me.

In the term euthanasia, "eu" means good, and "thanatose" means death. Euthanasia means death with dignity as it applies.

I remember my years in the ministry and being with families as they maintained a vigil, often 24 hours a day, with a dying loved one as if they would feel guilty if they were not present when the loved one passed away. Surely, they did not want anything that would shorten the time spent or rush the death. It was also a time for waiting for confessions; for saying the good things to each other that we so often feel, but so seldom voice until we are in the valley of the shadow of death. Then it was hoped that the physicians would do everything in their power to keep the loved one alive.

This has changed with the advent of modern medical technology. This change has brought another aspect of dying, or the direct intervention to terminate life called merciful death; the right of the person who is terminally ill to terminate his life and to free him from painful suffering; and to free the family from watching the slow death and of the draining of the family's financial resources.

Daniel McGuire in his article "Death—Legal and Illegal"[3] makes this bold statement. "The law of the land, any land, allows for killing as a legitimate activity." Boy, that's putting it heavy, putting it boldly right out front.

The Gallup Poll reflected a major shift in attitude on the subject of mercy killing. The question asked back in 1950 and again in 1973 was, "When a person has a disease that cannot be cured, do you think doctors should be allowed by law to end a person's life by some painless means, if the patient and his family request it?"

In 1950, only 36 percent said yes to the question. In 1973, 53 percent replied in the affirmative. Daniel C.

McGuire further commented on the statistical breakdown which revealed that among adults under 30 years of age the approval figure was 67 percent.

It is of interest to know that only 46 percent of the Roman Catholics interviewed said they disapproved; 48 percent said they approved and only 6 percent said they weren't sure. That means that not even a majority of Roman Catholics voice disapproval of mercy killing.

The four ways of ending life which have been legal in the eyes of at least some in this country are: Abortion, capital punishment, war and suicide. Mercy killing is still illegal. The courts have not given us a solid basis on which to evaluate mercy killing and have it clarified. It is still legally murder.

But in case after case, the courts and the juries rush to the plea of insanity at the time of the mercy killing, and then judge the person sane now. The courts, though, have not always acted the same way on mercy killing, and have sent a person to prison.

The physician is often confronted with a request just to leave some lethal medicine, enough for an overdose. If he leaves the medication available to his patient, is he guilty of murder? Or is he only guilty if he administers the medication himself or injects an air bubble into the patient's veins?

The law of Switzerland provides that whoever, from selfish motives, assists someone to commit suicide shall be punishable. If the motives are not selfish, then there will be no punishment. This means that a physician who is motivated by compassion and assists his patient to commit suicide is not subject to punishment.

How we will take a stand on the issue of mercy killing

and the right for a terminally ill person to end his own life is a needed area of exploration for the medical and legal professions, for insurance companies and the general public. I'm sure you noticed that I did not use the term suicide, but the right for a terminally ill person to end his own life.

Ever since St. Augustine, the Christian church has been hung up about suicide. Is it, or is it not, an unforgivable sin? Sometimes the terminally ill person's last act of love for his survivors is the ending of his life. One of the finest pamphlets I have ever read is entitled "Let's Talk about Death"[4] which quotes from a letter written to his doctors and nurses by Ronald Klingerbiel, a thirteen-year-old boy dying of leukemia:

> *I am dying. No one likes to talk about such things. In fact no one likes to talk about much at all, but I am the one who is dying! I know you feel insecure and don't know what to say and don't know what to do. But please believe me, if you care you can't go wrong. Just admit that you care—this is what we search for. We may ask for why's and wherefore's, but really don't want answers. Don't run away! Wait. All I want to know is will there be someone to hold my hand when I need it! I'm afraid; I've never died before.*

There is also the question, "Should the terminally ill patient know the truth about the finality of his illness?" I think in some cases, it is the right of the person to know and in others you would want to consider very carefully how the person would react to this knowledge. When they find out some give up immediately on life.

I believe that each patient, whether he has actually been told or not, eventually reaches his own conclusion about his condition.

Dr. Elisabeth Kübler-Ross wrote about the stages of dying in her book *On Death and Dying.*[5]

The first stage is that of denial. "No, not me!" This is the typical reaction. Denial is important and necessary because it helps cushion the shock and impact to the awareness that death is inevitable.

The second stage is rage and anger. "Why me?" The person resents the fact that others remain healthy and alive, while he must die. God is often a natural target for this anger. Unfortunately God is all too often seen as the causative agent in a person's death. To those who are shocked, Dr. Kübler-Ross replies that such anger is not only permissible but inevitable. "God can take it."

The next stage is bargaining with God—"Yes, me, but . . ." The person accepts the fact of death but tries to bargain for more time. Even a person who never believed in God now starts bargaining with Him. He promises to be good or do something in exchange for another week, a month or year of life. Dr. Kübler-Ross points out that what he promises is totally irrelevant because he wouldn't keep his promise anyway.

The fourth stage is that of depression. "Yes, me!" The person mourns past losses, things not done and wrongs committed. Then he enters a stage of preparatory grief, quietly getting ready for the arrival of the stranger, Death. The person withdraws into a stage of quietness and does not care for any visitors. "When a dying person doesn't want to see you any more," says Dr. Kübler-Ross, "this is a sign he has finished his unfinished business with you, and it is a blessing. He can now let go peacefully."

The final stage is that of acceptance. "My time is very close now, and it's all right." Dr. Kübler-Ross describes this final stage as neither a happy stage nor an unhappy one. It's devoid of feeling, but it is not resignation. It's somewhat akin to victory. I have often noticed a sense of euphoria, a flight into health, in the last stages of a cancer patient. "I'm going to make it after all!" This does not mean, "I am going to get well." I finally decided it means "I'm ready for the last frontier—Death."

The reactions of those who are survivors can range from stoic denial to a rage against God, or even against the loved one who died.

There was a man who went to a graveyard every evening after work, sobbed at a graveside, pounded on the grave, and said over and over, "Why did you have to die? Why did you have to die?"

Since his grief was not easing up after the passage of many weeks, the caretaker went to offer the grieving man his comfort. He said, "Never in all my years of being a caretaker at the cemetery have I ever experienced such grief as yours. You must have loved that person very much."

"No. Why did you have to die? Why did you have to die?"

"Well, who could it have been that you loved so much?"

"I didn't love that person so much," he replied.

"Then who was it that died?"

"My wife's first husband," he sobbed. "Why did you have to die?"

Seriously, one of the most difficult if not impossible questions to answer, is "Why?" Too often people search for a way to make sense of death; to make it have a purpose of a matter of justice. It's hard to accept the fact that death is not a matter of God's will, but an act of life. We are born mortal and are vulnerable to disease from the moment we enter this world, and death is our final destiny. These are facts. And remember, death is not fair.

Here are some guidelines to help people through the grief experience.

(1) Be there with the bereaved, and remember you don't know how it feels for him personally. Don't feel compelled to give him any answers. Accept your limitations, but let him know that you're there and don't know what to say, but don't want him to be alone.

(2) Allow the bereaved to cry and express his anger, his ambivalence and his sorrow. When in doubt as to what to say, shut up! And listen!

(3) Accept his grief and reassure him that it is normal, and that maybe only time will be the healer.

(4) Remember even a person who thinks that he is prepared for the loss of a loved one, especially an elderly parent, finds himself still unprepared for the loss when it comes. Don't try to minimize his loss because age really doesn't matter.

(5) See what you can do to help, by doing small errands, or finding out who you can contact for him. Help him plan an orderly course of events for the next few days.

(6) This is very important. Plan to visit him and talk

over honestly the grief experience about three weeks after the funeral. This is the time when the full impact of the loss has hit a person, there is no one there, and the hectic activity of preparing for a funeral, greeting friends and relatives and making decisions is long past. Everyone has returned to his normal pace of life. Now he is alone with grief and with his shock and melancholy. Then is when you can love through listening to let him know that you are there when he needs to talk and to know that someone still cares.

Personally and privately, I feel that funeral homes and mortuaries serve an important service to families in time of death. What I'm about to say is not meant as an indictment against morticians, but rather as an alternative to the normal way funerals are conducted. This is how I would want my funeral to be conducted, and is by no means a guideline for anyone else but me.

First of all, there would be no public showing of an open casket, but soon after I die there would be a private committal service at the graveside, very brief, for family and close friends. I would like a memorial service to be held in my church. There would be no sad songs, only the music of Easter such as "I Know That My Redeemer Liveth." If possible a choir would sing the "Hallelujah Chorus" from Handel's *Messiah*. This would not be a time of grief, but a celebration of God's victory over death. I would want no long eulogy but a meditation about God's love that was so great that it led to Calvary; about God's power which was so great that Christ was raised from the dead on Easter, and God's promise that the final resurrection will come to pass with the saying, "When death is swallowed up in victory, Oh death, where is thy victory. Oh death, where is thy sting?"[6]

These are my own personal feelings and beliefs and if you disagree, and see things differently, then that is your right. All I am saying is that this is how I have come to terms with death personally. This is something each person must do for himself.

How to Add Life to Your Years and Not Just Years to Your Life.

Due to the advances in modern medicine, do you realize that the average human life span in the United States has increased from 48 years in 1900 to about 70 in 1975? It is not too unrealistic to say that life expectancy may soon be 100 years.

What would happen to life expectancies if by some miracle breakthrough, cancer and heart disease were eliminated? Have you ever wondered how much extra life that would mean? Precious little, according to scientists. Two years additional for cancer and seven years more for heart disease. Thus, a generation of humans in which two major causes of death were eliminated would surprisingly add only nine or ten additional years of life. Says Dr. Leonard Hayflick, a distinguished microbiologist, "I don't think anyone has ever died of old age! There is always one part that wears out first, and wrecks the whole human machinery."

I wonder if it has ever occurred to you that why I started out talking about death? Wouldn't it have been more logical to talk about growing old and aging first, and then talk about death? It may be logical, but psychologically I believe that making peace with death and having death as an advisor helps guide our way to a full life. Honestly many of us don't need to grow old, but to grow up.

Karl Menninger once said in a conference in Phoenix that, "Adolescence begins with the onset of puberty and ends with the acquisition of wisdom." It is no great achievement to stay alive for a number of years. What is important is to find a quality to your life, to always be growing and to maintain a zest for life. You must find ways to express yourself, not just in work, but also in thanksgiving and gratitude.

How long do you expect to live? Ask someone in the Caucasus Mountains of Russia and the answer will be about three hundred.[7] He never doubts that he will make it to at least one hundred. If you ask the average person in the United States how long he expects to live, the answer will be between sixty and seventy.

Several years ago, Dr. Alexander Lief of the Harvard Medical School and Chief of Medical Services in Massachusetts General Hospital, took a leisurely trip to the lands where people commonly live to one hundred or more. To his utter amazement he found very thin centenarians and very fat ones; those who ate too much, drank too much and smoked too much. Yet they were alive and vigorous at a fantastic age. How could this be? This question haunted Dr. Lief, because he was sold on the importance of low-fat, low-calorie intake, low-cholesterol diets. Yet in these faraway lands evidence was to the contrary.

The secret had to be in their attitude. According to Dr. Lief, if you're not put on the shelf, if you're not cast aside, and if you remain as a respected, participatory member of society, you are motivated to keep going. Dr.

Robert Samp, a Milwaukee physician who studied 130 American centenarians, noted that almost all of them had the uncanny ability to throw off disagreeable incidents.

Now do you believe that the secret of life is turning off negative tapes, and not being controlled emotionally by the actions of other people or events? Negative tapes are truly a drag and a parasite on life. Also, all the studies of Dr. Samp show that marriage and long life (like old wine and good cheese) are a perfect match.

Exercises that keep the machine in good condition are important. A curious mind that is always willing to grow and learn keeps a mind alive. Following good nutrition keeps a body healthy and able to repair itself. Having good humor and the ability to laugh at yourself is another important secret.

As I have noted earlier, the United States is obsessed with youth, and its energy and aggressiveness. This leaves litle room for thinking about the aged and aging. To be old commands little respect. It is too often synonymous with being old fashioned and out of touch. Businesses sometimes force very vital and alive men into a forced retirement that kills them.

There is a story about a young married couple with a five-year-old son. The husband's father, who lived with them, had a case of palsy, and his hands would shake while he was eating so that some food would slip from his mouth and spill on his napkin. He was scolded for being sloppy and messy, and was told to stop or he couldn't eat at the table with them. One night the old gentleman spilled again and his son was furious. "You eat like a pig! It makes me sick to watch you eat. Since you eat like a pig, I'll make you a trough." On Saturday his son made him a trough and placed it in the kitchen, faced his father to the wall and told him he would have to eat from the trough like a pig. A few days later the young husband and wife noticed their five-year-old son carving something out of wood. They asked him what he was making and he replied, "Oh, I'm practicing making a trough for you when you grow old." Stunned by the open honesty of their son, and deeply ashamed, they threw away the trough and invited grandpa back to the dining room table for their evening meals. For some reason his palsy and his spills and dirty napkin didn't seem to bother them so much anymore.

I wish there could be more ways for our senior citizens to feel needed by helping in schools and having people listen to their stories. Sometimes I even have fantasies of a TV or radio show which would be written and produced by senior citizens on which they could tell their stories, read their poetry, exhibit their art and humor and aliveness. I think that if we could listen to the wisdom of the aged, we would mature much sooner.

Don't you love to hear the stories of someone who has lived through so much in their life? I am thrilled to see people, no matter how old, trying new ideas. I am awed by people who still have a tremendous zest for life and respond always to its challenge. Their secret of life is in their love of people. I would like to share with you this poem by Gerald McArthur.

AGING

Nobody grows old by merely living a number of years,
People grow old only by deserting their ideals

*You are as young as your self-confidence, as old as
    your fear,
As young as your hope, and as old your despair.
In the central place of every heart, there is a
    recording chamber
So long as it receives messages of beauty, hope, cheer
    and courage
So long are you young.
When the wires are all down and your heart is
    covered
With the snows of pessimism, the ice of cynicism,
Then, and only then, are you grown old.*

THE PSYCHOLOGY OF HOPE

*It's better to light one candle,
than to curse the darkness . . .*
Chinese Proverb

The psychology of hope is believing in people, and realizing that people have within themselves the power to change. Hope is trusting people to grow in beauty, creativity, sensitivity and aliveness. The basis of a person's life is hope. Where there is hope, there is life—and not the other way around. When there is no hope for the future, there is no power for the present. Once the candle of hope is extinguished, the road is all downhill.

I have hope for our country and its future. I'm a little tired of the adulation and praise we bestow upon the critics of our times who receive a ready and appreciative audience when they tell us over and over how bad our country is. Although the severest critics speak of how rotten life is, they have not left to live in another country.

I admit we do have problems, but we're a nation noted

for its ability to solve problems. We get complacent and lulled by our luxury, but finally when things become painful and we awaken out of our lethargy, we are again a nation of great technological and creative ability.

On the editor's page of the *U.S. News and World Report* Howard Flieger wrote an editorial called "A Case Against Gloom."[1]

The basis of his editorial is a book by Ben J. Wattenberg, *The Real America*. Mr. Wattenberg is a serious economic and social analyst who has studied the statistics of the U.S. Census, of public opinion polls, and industrial, academic and market surveys. He has reached some very interesting conclusions. "The dominant rhetoric of our time is a rhetoric of failure, guilt and crises . . . The evidence of the data is the evidence of progress, growth and success."

Here are a few of the statistical examples: "Real family income after inflation has doubled in a generation . . . Fringe benefits, job equities that don't show up in a pay envelope, advanced from 23.4 billion dollars in 1960 to 79.7 billion in 1972, and they are still growing . . . By official definition, a fifth of all Americans were living in poverty in 1959. Now the total is half that . . . College enrollment in 1960 was about 3.5 million. By 1973, college enrollment had reached 8.6 million, and it is estimated to exceed 10 million by 1980 . . . Furthermore, about 60 percent of today's college students come from families in which the head of the household has never even completed one year of college. Among blacks, the figure goes up to 80 percent . . . The number of women in the professions has gone up sharply. There has been a great increase in the percent of women in the total

labor force, even though some of the women's lib movements may not want to own up to it . . . Americans start
working later, put in fewer hours, and retire earlier."

Do you realize that the United States, according to an
economist friend of mine, has now reached the point
where the middle class composes approximately 80 percent of our population with 10 percent as the wealthy and
10 percent as the poor or below-middle class. This is the
largest middle-class society in history.

What is the middle class doing with its hard-earned
money? Well, it's not being as recklessly spent as you
think. Figures in Wattenberg's book show that the greatest
increases in family spending are on education, health,
recreation and housing. Less money is spent on cos-
metics, alcohol and jewelry. Mr. Wattenberg says, "The
point is that, given a vast increase in discretionary income over the last decade, the broad spending trends have
been commonsensical and worthwhile."

The heroes of this fascinating book, are the American
people who are smarter, wiser, calmer and shrewder,
tougher and more forgiving than either the critics of the
right or the left.

Mr. Wattenberg, in digesting all the data of two dec-
ades, sketches his hero as resourceful, adaptable and independent, but depicts him as a chronic complainer. He
prophesies for the future that Americans will continue
to complain about their lot and will go right on progress-
ing.

Do you think that what you believe is often what you
receive? If you believe that life is rotten and that people
are no good, your chances are very high of ending up
with the "no-goods of life."

Even more important, a psychology of hope need to be emphasized in the field of mental health. Mental health professionals too often stress mental illness and diagnostic categories. Even the term mental illness is destructive. It only makes the problems of coping with life and our emotions a matter of sickness. It's as though here is a mental illness germ and it's a disgrace to catch it. It also tends to absolve you from personal responsibility for your health, and to rely on somebody else or medication to solve the problem. With all the pills that Americans have swallowed to give them tranquillity and peace medication has still not been the answer. Furthermore, when a person engages in lengthy psychotherapy and spends a year or two focusing on the mistakes of the past, it is a wonder that anyone ever gets better. I wonder when we are going to learn that we can't change yesterday, so why dwell on yesterday's mistakes?

I believe that people are too often over-medicated and zonked. The message, overtly or covertly implied, says that if you stop taking the medicine you will go crazy. So even if you do make some positive changes in your life, it's the pills and the doctor that get the credit instead of you.

A person still looks for answers, and goes from doctor to doctor until finally, one says, "Well, there is nothing more I can do for you." Where do you go now? If you have given personal responsibility to the professional to heal you, it's as if the rug of hope is pulled out from under you.

A Psychology of Hope means that you have the power within yourself to change. Hope is a personal decision, not reached during the bright and sunny days when all

is well with your world and you feel the joy and exulta-
tion of everything coming up roses.

Hope is not called for in the ordinary days when life
just seems to bump along on its same routine. Hope is
a decision made in the darknes of life, where there is pain
and despair, and often in the shadow of death.

Hope is a decision when there seems to be little evidence to support that decision. In fact the evidence
may point heavily in the opposite direction, which might
make a person decide, "I quit. I give up. I can't go on
any longer."

Hope is like hearing a bird singing in the darkness in
anticipation of the dawn. Hope is also born of a decision
to stop thinking that other people can make it right with
your life. It's letting go of the destructive, heavy burdens
of bitterness, hate, fear and guilt, and saying, "Here I
am, God help me."

The final source of my hope is my relationship with
God. I know that if you have stayed with me to this
point, you are aware that I am not writing about topics.
The writing is a form of communication between me and
you. To communicate effectively with you, I have tried to
be open with you about who I am. I know you have the
right to disagree with the statements I have made. That's
only normal.

If I were to continue to reveal myself to you, it would
mean that I would have to share my own personal religious faith because it's a vital part of me. I hope you realize
that I have not said you have to see the world my way or
even have a religious faith. That's a very personal decision for you.

A living faith in God, has been a part of my life ever

since I was a little child. My childlike faith in God used to worry my mother. I had such faith as a child that if anything ever went wrong with me, God would just slide down a rope and pull me out. My mother kept worrying that I would put the rope theory to the ultimate test.

When I was six years old my family went to a vacation in Estes Park, Colorado. What a beautiful uncluttered natural wonderland the Rockies were in 1936. A party of us had taken a long hike into the back countries to visit some of the lakes. Somehow coming back on the trail that afternoon, the group was split into two groups. All of a sudden I realized that I was with neither group and it was getting late in the afternoon. I was lost.

Having the faith of a child, I prayed to God about what I should do. He told me to stay right where I was, so I sat down on a rock by the trail and waited.

When the two groups of people joined forces for the hike down the mountain, they suddenly realized I was not with either group. Frantically they raced up the mountain fearing that I had strayed off the trail. Everyone was relieved to see me sitting on a rock waiting for them.

When I was asked how I knew enough to stay where I was, I told them that I had prayed, and God had told me what to do. I was surprised they even had to ask!

I wish I could report to you that my trust in God continued to be so real and vital to me. I found that my personal faith went in cycles. Sometimes it was very real and alive; other times I would drift and God seemed very far away. Maybe it was the thrill of getting things done for myself that made me count more and more on myself. Then I would again find a deep yearning within myself to get things squared away with God.

I often think that some of the hard times in my spiritual life were just ordinary days when I felt a need for God. Yet there were other times when I would be in trouble and would anxiously seek an answer through prayer. I hoped for some personal experience or sign that God was alive and real. When I found that God was silent, it was hard to accept and to keep on believing.

One of the most inspirational men I have ever known is William Wallner. He had grown up in Europe and had become a Lutheran minister in Prague, Czechoslovakia. At first his congregation was small, but not for long. If ever God used a man, He used Dr. Wallner. Hitler was coming to power in Germany and soon Wallner was preaching five sermons on Sunday to over 25,000 people in different languages. In his parish were over 3,000 Jews, including a rabbi, who had become Christians. This was an unusual ministry, caring for refugees who came by the thousands to escape Hitler. One of these was a talented and proud young Jewish man named Karl Loes from Frankfurt. He had been an outstanding drama and art critic, and his word could make or break a beginning star. He told Dr. Wallner he did not want to become a Christian, and was embarrassed to ask for help. However, he did become a Christian, and a powerful leader with university students. When Hitler came to Czechoslovakia Karl fled for his life and Wallner lost track of him.

Pastor Wallner stayed as long as he could in Czechoslovakia. He accomplished an heroic action when he discovered that a number of Jewish children were to be taken out in the cold of December and left to freeze to death in a ditch. Quickly Pastor Wallner arranged through the underground to have the Allies fly them out to safety under the noses of the Nazis. He has been honored by having an olive grove planted in his honor by the State of Israel.

At the end of the war a group of underground fighters were discovered in a cellar and were all murdered by the Nazis who left in disorganized retreat. On the walls were messages written in various languages, and Wallner was asked to translate them. One of the poems stopped him cold, for this is what he read:

> *I believe in the sun when it is not shining.*
> *I believe in love, when I do not feel it.*
> *I believe in my Lord, Jesus, even when he is silent.*

It was signed *Karl Loes*. Wallner wept at this last tragic meeting with his long-lost friend, but there was also wonderment at the faith of this man who had soared to such great heights.

The God I believe in is not a God of fear or of death. I do not blame God for my mistakes—or the mistakes of mankind. I believe in a God of Hope—a God of Love and a God of Forgiveness. And a God so amazing and creative that it overwhelms me.

Once again, I am a child of faith, in awe of the God of Life.

"All human wisdom is summed up in two words—wait and hope."

Alexander Dumas, the elder

REFERENCE NOTES

CHAPTER 2

1. Hugh Prather. *Notes to myself*. Moab, Utah: Real People Press, 1970.

CHAPTER 3

1. Ralph G. Nichols and Leonard A. Stevens. *Are You Listening?* New York: McGraw-Hill Book Company, 1957

2. Gerald I. Nierenberg. *The Art of Negotiating*. New York: Cornerstone Library, 1968.

3. Reuel L. Howe. *The Miracle of Dialogue*. New York: The Seabury Press, 1963.

4. Vance Packard. *The Hidden Persuaders*. New York: Pocket Books, Inc., 1957.

5. John Powell. *Why Am I Afraid To Tell You Who I Am?* Niles, Ill.: Argus Communications, 1969.

6. Feodor Dostoevsky. *The Brothers Karamazov*. New York: The Modern Library, 1950.

7. Paul Watzlawick. *An Anthology of Human Communication* (Audio Tape). Palo Alto: Science and Behavior Books, Inc., 1964.

   Virginia Satir. *Conjoint Family Therapy*. Palo Alto: Science and Behaviors Books, Inc., 1964.

   Paul Watzlawick, Janet Beavin and Don D. Jackson. *Pragmatics of Human Communication*. New York: W.W. Norton & Co., Inc. 1967.

   Jay Haley. *Strategies of Psychotherapy*. New York: Grune and Stratton, 1963.

   Don D. Jackson, Editor. *Communication, Family and Mar-*

riage. Vol. 1. Palo Alto: Science and Behavior Books, Inc., 1968.

Don D. Jackson. *Therapy, Communication and Change.* Palo Alto: Science and Behavior Books, Inc., 1968.

8. Don D. Jackson. "The Study of the Family," *Family Process Magazine.* 1965, 4 (1).

9. R.D. Laing, H. Phillipson and A.R. Lee. *Interpersonal Perception: A Theory and a Method of Research.* London: Tavistock Publications, New York: Springer, 1966.

10. Robert Townsend. *Up the Organization.* New York: Knopf, 1970.

CHAPTER 4

1. Kenneth J. Olson. "An Investigation of Scapegoating, Favoritism and Self-Blame in Families." Ph.D. dissertation, Arizona State University, 1968.

2. J. Frazer. *The Golden Bough.* New York: MacMillan, 1927.

CHAPTER 9

1. Victor Frankl. *Man's Search for Meaning: An Introduction to Logo Therapy.* New York: Washington Square Press, 1963, p. 122.

2. T.S. Eliot, "Choruses from the Rock," *The Complete Poems and Plays.* New York: Harcourt, Brace & Company, 1934, p. 96.

3. Matthew 6: 25-27

4. John 5: 2-9

5. Patrick Young. "Preventive Dentistry—No More Drilling, Filling, Billing?" *The National Observer.* 17 June 1972.

6. John Yudkin. *Sweet and Dangerous.* New York: Peter H. Wyden, Inc., 1972.

7. Clair Pierre. "The Nutrition Dilemma," *Saturday Review World.* 1974.

8. Roger Williams. *Nutrition Against Disease.* New York: Pitman Publishing Corporation, 1971.

9. E. Cheraskin, W.M. Ringsdorf and Arline Brecher. *Psycho-Dietetics.* New York: Stein and Day, 1974.

10. Hans Selye. *The Stress of Life.* New York: McGraw-Hill and Company, 1956.

11. Meyer Friedman and Ray H. Rosenman. *Type A Behavior and Your Heart.* New York: Knopf, 1974.

CHAPTER 10

1. T.S. Eliot. "Choruses from the Rock," *The Complete Poems and Plays*. New York: Harcourt, Brace and Company, 1934, p. 104.

2. Carlos Castaneda. *Journey to Ixtlan*. New York: Simon and Schuster, 1972, p. 54.

3. Daniel C. Maguire. "Death—Legal and Illegal," *Vesper Exchange*, No. 2360, June, 1974.

4. "Let's Talk About Death," *Christopher News Notes*. New York: No. 206.

5. Elizabeth Kübler-Ross. *On Death and Dying*. New York: MacMillan Publishing Company, Inc., 1970.

6. I Corinthians 15: 54-55.

7. Norman Meinick. "You Don't Have to Grow Old Before Your Time," *Mainliner*. Vol. 19, No. 1, January 1975.

CHAPTER 11

1. Howard Flieger. "A Case Against Gloom," *U.S. News and World Report*. March 17, 1975.